Tony Blair
and the
Ideal Type

J.H. Grainger

IMPRINT ACADEMIC

Published in the UK by Imprint Academic
PO Box 200, Exeter EX5 5YX, UK

Published in the USA by Imprint Academic
Philosophy Documentation Center
PO Box 7147, Charlottesville, VA 22906-7147, USA

ISBN 1 84540 024 0

A CIP catalogue record for this book is available from the
British Library and US Library of Congress

Foreword

The New Labour party that triumphed at the General Election of 1997 exhaled the lost promise of politics but steered clear of specific political promises. What it brought forth were not programmes but broad intentions. From the beginning it was presented as the lengthening shadow of one man, Tony Blair, possessed of superior 'values' and general ideas of all kinds. Grounded therefore neither in intellectual theory nor in history but in a longing for 'things to be different', dedicated to 'modernity' in culture, social and political structure and, above all, in the conduct of politics itself, the project of New Labour, with echoes from both the defunct Social Democratic Party and the small but extant Liberal Democrat Party, stood for co-operation not conflict among competing political parties, amity not enmity in society. In the arrangements of politics Blair despised the wisdom of the ancients, disparaged the 'ages' hard-bought gain' or what Attlee, a very different politician, had once called 'the mess of centuries'.

It is indeed, at first sight, surprising to find this passion for making things new — for pitting what turned out to be this simple political or utilitarian rationalism against what had been used and proved over time — by one who in some ways appeared to be a political romantic. For romanticism, we learn, lies not in the object contemplated, the individual, the age, the venture, the departure, the victory or the project, but in the subject himself using what 'occasions' are available or conjurable to create from wish or dream imagined 'realities', alternatives to those which diurnally persist. From such displacement politics moves to a higher plane on which harmony ensues. Whether or not in the *Weltanschauung* of, say, Blair all innovations, transformations and departures are reconciled within his romantic self or there persist anomalies, disjunctions and contradictions, there can be little doubt about the eclecticism of his conduct or politics. As prime actor and mover his states of mind observe no frontiers. At the same time it seems that he is utterly convinced of his own chameleonically derived insights into his own times and the validity of his political judgments. He is unlikely to concur with the perception of Hans Georg Gadamer that:

> The self-awareness of the individual is only a flickering in the closed circuits of historical life. That is why the prejudices of the individual, far more than his judgments, constitute the historical reality of his being.

'Blairism' was to consist of the development of a moment for renewal, political, social and spiritual. As in 1906 and 1945, 'the people' were persuaded that something was happening. Yet Blair was a leader qualitatively other than either Campbell-Bannerman or Attlee. Throughout his campaign from Labour leadership to the Election, his appeal was to the emergent; he was the chosen vehicle of what was to come. The historic purpose of Labour, writes Ben Pimlott, was sloughed off 'like a snakeskin without growing another that is no more substantial than mere consumer responsiveness'. Ascriptions, labels, derivations and lineages — 'New Liberal', 'Social Democrat', 'Christian Socialist', 'Ethical Socialist' — fell away from him like leaves from a tree. Ideas, inert or ineffective, such as 'Social-ism' as a substitute for 'Socialism' proved to be unargued, unconcluded counters, rapidly consumed or left for dead in the flame of what John Lloyd called his 'bombastic, emotionally promiscuous, hubristic' platform rhetoric. Blair has no settled views even on 'stake-holding', that much bruited social democratic specific of European (and Singaporean) provenance in which the merits of the market and the virtues of the civic order were to be merged so as to yoke the energies and efficacies of commerce to the ends of social cohesion in Blair's version of 'one nation'. None of them mattered much to one deeply engaged in the projection of values rather than the prescriptions of an ideology.

It may be that Blair was wary of specific political action because it demanded both practical, effective knowledge about the workings of society to which we never seem to attain and conspiring circumstances which seldom turn up. Perhaps, despite his early rhetoric, he doubted his own prowess in the face of dire possibility of proof of the fact remarked by Andreas Schedler that 'the capacity to act has migrated out of the political system', that in the event fears would triumph over hopes. A vision that merely insists that *things can be different* and is intent on transcending the obstructive present by adversely comparing it with what does not yet exist, some ineffable future state, requires neither knowledge nor specifics. To invoke his dream, to move or bore us with it, the visionary needs only an ardent, tirelessly active personality, histrionic gifts and some inspiring language so that he may soar above the endlessly, tiresome repertory of routine politics.

At a time when the two 'great parties' seemed stale and earthbound in their stock hostilities such future-orientated high-mindedness enabled Blair eclectically to attract to his own untrammelled subjectivity such footloose allegiances (himself, he had none), edifications and tutelages from which there might be fashioned for the unpersuaded or uncommitted a new political centre movement or party akin to the former Social Democratic Party, but, on this occasion, developing not from deep within but as a revolution from above by a circle at the very apex of the Labour party. Through Blair the excluded middle would at last take on a formation capable of seizing and holding power. From whatever became detached from other formations he would yoke together what seemed useful to him.

As romantic, political emanation — perhaps only a fleeting essence — Blair was not predisposed to accept the limitations of politics. He was embarking on something that was 'important to our future as human beings'. New Labour would 'progress to explore new frontiers of human achievement' — achievements to be shared by all nations, 'just not our own'. Like earlier platform orators of Scottish provenance, Gladstone, Rosebery and MacDonald, he sought to move his audience not so much by argument as by 'elevation', by undetailed moral fervour. Within the darkness of the political theatre, they became prisoners of his grace. There, on the illumined stage, he gave moment and drama to political choice; for political artifice he conferred new 'community' on the serried stalls; they saw 'a great man' in the making, a politician strenuously playing the part so that he might become the part.

At the Labour party Conference in October 1996 he made a Covenant with Britain which, to editorial and arch-episcopal approval, 'the People' sealed at the next General Election. Thus he was pledged to deliver the realm by mighty acts from the encumbrance of the past. 'I give you my word.' So he committed himself against intangible, inimical forces to an infinitely broader and more ethereal field for action than any envisaged by Mrs Thatcher, owned as his leading mentor in ideas and practice. At the next party Conference, at last in power, he confirmed his transforming purpose:

> Today, I issue a challenge to you. Help us make Britain that beacon shining throughout the world united behind a mission to modernize our country. Believe in us as much as we believe in you. Give just as much to our country as we intend to give. Give your all. Make this the giving age.

Not even Lloyd George loosed himself upon the country in so Messianic a manner. The great creative campaigns of Gladstone and Joseph Chamberlain had been centred upon specific cause or issue. They were not personal ventures into the open future.

As covenanted promise-maker Blair bases the success of his enterprise upon public trust in his moral character and faith in the efficacy of his agency. He is the singular man: confidently, he assumes burdens that would break other politicians' backs. To the speaking, exciting present belong the reconciliations of mind and heart, pledges of constructive engagements and settlements, removal of impediments and deadlocks in domestic, European and world politics. To the active, exacting future are consigned the equivocations, complicities, dissemblings and 'hard choices'. For today, the familiar invocation of hope against fear, the insistence that there is a 'vision within our grasp'.

This last shines not at all from 'the lamp of experience' but is lit rather by the religio-political discursiveness of the undergraduate. Like the animated undergraduate, he finds it difficult, without instruction, to take a political stance. So he strikes attitudes, climbs into pulpits and discovers his vocation as an evangelist, as a spell-binder: one who imbues others with enthusiasm and purpose while himself remaining without clear political identity. His language is attuned in accent, syntax and tone to both audience and occasion. All things to all men, he is indeed an 'occasionalist' making what he wills out of what is before him: an expectant party conference, a focus or pop group, a memorial service for the celebrated dead. The captive audience is always an opportunity for projecting himself, for 'charm' and persuasion, for charging others with his outflowing energy; he is indeed 'the genial ego'. His grace ensures that there need be no argument, sometimes, perhaps, not too much sense. Thus Blair achieves leadership, office and power without resolving his indeterminacy, without defining either loyalties or enmities. There are no frontiers, external or internal. There is no motive but the achievement of his own *réclame*.

Out of this unclouded openness to both novelty and redemption, the leadership of New Labour, desperately seeking office, found itself obliged, despite its eschewal of 'ideology' to send signals of general aims and direction to the political nation — the crescent, unpolitical nation cared for little but presence and presentation — if only to bestow coherence and consistency upon Blair himself in speech and action. New Labour had to be explained as an ideal and as a way so that Blairism might aspire to leave the same formative stamp on the country as had Thatcherism in all its didactic simplicity. What resulted from this belated doctrine-hunting of a doctrine-less *politique* was something less than an ideology; rather a gloss upon and a glossary for intentions and action.

Following conventional wisdom the chosen path for action was in the middle, between capitalism and socialism, between New Right and Old Labour. Although this Third Way constituted neither thesis nor antithesis it was, in substance, a critique of what had been achieved and an application of certain maxims, nostrums, valuable attitudes of varying provenance to the Thatcherite going concern. There was little that was novel in the *mélange* of ideas, ideals, watchwords and techniques that was intended to endorse or modify what had worked under Thatcher. Nor was there anything notably running counter to the continuities of British politics. Characteristically, the Third Way built bridges, sought to achieve consensus or partnership between the claims of the community and the interests of the individual, between the responsibilities of citizens and their rights; in particular, between the public and the private in industry and commerce, between public and voluntary services in the social sphere. Beyond that, it stood for the indefatigable exploitation of the 'knowledge economy', the fostering of 'human capital' and entrepreneurial 'creativity' in the pursuit of insular wealth, the abandonment of taxolatry and re-distribution as axes of public policy. Above all, of course, it pitted the modern against the given, against the inequity and the iniquity of the *status quo*. Yet the end in fact — apart from the acquisition of the trappings of office and the long-withheld satisfaction of personal ambitions — proved to be little more than the achievement of that competence which political predecessors had allegedly failed to exhibit during their lease of authority.

All these prescriptions presupposed amity and cooperation; they did not divide either voters or parties into friends and enemies; thus, they gainsaid the essence of the political. Yet they portended a recognizably left-of-centre, active state faithfully effecting 'tough' economic and social policies, unrelenting intervention, much of it 'hands-on', in schools, hospitals and the like; a tutelary executive government of inspectors, commissioners, 'namers and shamers', loosing messages and messengers, boasting steely intentions and cutting edges. But above all, the Third Way predicated moral leadership of the whole nation, government through the inspiration of a single, autonomous person — the irresistible victor of the electoral battlefield.

This New Labour project, righteous and redeeming, was not to be confined to one parliamentary term. The inspiration would continue. 'We were elected as New Labour and will govern as New Labour.' No longer were General Elections to be, in Namier's words, 'locks on the canal of English history'. The blessed regime would take over for a generation. 'For I do not want a one-term Labour government that dazzles for a moment then ends in disillusion. I want a Labour government that governs for a generation and changes Britain for good.' Notice the absence of the royal or party 'we'. There is only the singular heroic energy of a Fichtean ego wishing to make something, it knows not what, of the world, rejoicing in the autonomy given through its mastery of the liberal-democratic state, specifically exulting in the possibility of changing the course of history, perhaps of fashioning a new-style 'elect nation', necessarily within rather than outside a puissant European Union. What this posture recalls is not the intent-laden, single-eyed able statesman moving with tide and time, periodically demanded since Edwardian times to restore purpose and power to a declining realm. Rather, Blair calls up, as ideal type, the Promethean Liberal leader from nineteenth-century Europe, the platform orator moved by an inner light, radical and transformative, persuasive and prophetic and at the same time prospective master of a sovereign parliament.

After the 1997 Election it seemed very likely that in Blair a commissioned dictator, a demagogue and plebiscitary opportunist had been raised to power. It was assumed that New Labour in government would remain as disciplined and obedient as it had been in opposition. The *eventum* of a firm, durable executive in full command of a grateful and deferential will-organization, all too eager to applaud 'a *prima donna assoluta* of statesmanship' on the floor of the Commons, was fully confirmed. Thus, through the loyalty and united will of a single 'great party', overjoyed to have any power at all, Blair would be enabled to carry out his own 'irreversible shift' towards a qualitative change in politics. What had been benign, ethereal promise would be practically realized through brute votes. Institutionally then 'Blairism' at the outset portended stable, unimpeded executive authority through prerogative powers as customarily vested in the office of the Prime Minister. The difference between Blair's and previous possibly comparable regimes lay in his confident claim to be in sole possession of unusual gifts of political inspiration, instigation and regeneration.

By political disposition as well as by what R.G. Collingwood called 'the dialectic of internal politics' Blair was moved beyond electoral conquest of to appeasement of and co-operation with political adversaries; to come to terms with their residual griev- ances and enmities, to weaken their allegiance to party and attract them into coalition or office, thus to absorb them by pref- erence or selection into his grand synthesis. At the same time Blair was always set to maintain his personal dominance as a 'rhetorical' first minister with assigned or deputed ministers and aides, a core circle of old and new committed *friends* who had recognized and invested in his mobilizing talents and public appeal. They informed both his tactics and his strategies but did not comprise a junta. Blair retained his status as prime mover. Without him, invocation of or reference to him, they were like uncharged batteries.

What was from the beginning notable was Blair's visibility, his ubiquity, his invasive alacrity, his quick, nervous affability, his ready opinionation and moral persuasion. You were, more- over, never allowed to forget his 'first fine careless rapture'. Staff and party acolytes — as well as receptive or complicit media — assiduously promoted or 'spun' both person and performance. From an indefatigable and overbearing Press Officer said to be virtually a co-ruler or a duumvir — surely not prepotent — in devising immediate responses from No 10, there came 'rapid rebuttal' of any untoward depreciation or deprecation of the actions or attitudes of the upstart mortal god. Ministers and ministerialists, Members of Parliament, were all subjected to the information and surveillance of 'pagers', monitors, informers, 'shadows' and 'castlers' by what looked very like a grand vizier and his omniscient staff all instrumental in enforcing the correct party line of the leadership.

Inside and outside Parliament, the will of the Prime Minister would be unhampered by party structures. Within the party, the National Executive Committee, with composition duly adjusted, would cease to be an apex of policy formulation — Blair insisted that he would not be held up 'by twenty men in a room'. Outside, in the country, the Annual Conference would lose its functions of fundamental criticism and counter-choice, even its time-honoured function of cumulatively contributing to party policy by composite resolutions and become a televised rally to cheer and celebrate the leadership.

With the reign of virtue would come a Barebones (i.e. largely novitiate) Parliament of dedicated would-be professional Members — many of them brands plucked from the burning by Blair himself — comprising no Commons of England/Britain assembled but a vast, if adventitious, support for the Legislator, a nescient, biddable Mountain of radical general values, gathered and harangued at the outset of the first session by the Prime Minister himself. Conduct, attendance and voting in chamber and committee were to be strictly monitored. They would be informed, 'paged' and prompted by invisible agencies. Dissidents or absentees would be identified by whips as 'malignants' and reproved. Those in the great following who were surplus to voting requirements in the division lobbies would be dispatched periodically to their seats not only the better to serve their constituents but also to act as 'ambassadors' for the vanguard in office and thus to secure for it a second term. Of electioneering there would be no end. Never before had there been such a close fusing of the conduct of government and politics.

For Blair to impose 'modernity' upon the country as quickly as he can he must use the sovereignty of Parliament to the full. For him, support in the House of Commons, larger than is necessary, cumbersome and possibly fissiparous, must become and remain one and undivided. Parliament is not to be a place of deferral, referral or half measures but a place for settlement, for the achievement of public purpose. He is not at ease there and has contempt for mere debate. He prefers to be responsive to the people on a public platform, at a rostrum or in a focus group and policy forum. Thus he fosters the old liberal nostrum of government by discussion. But this is misleading. In the end, like all would-be master-politicians, Blair desires not a dialogue but a monologue. What matters is the resolution of discussion by *force of persuasion*.

This then is Blair, the providential ruler, the Single Person, dependent upon the overwhelming strength of a single party for his domination of the political order. At need, he gives himself a label but remains undenominational. From polls and focus groups is educed a rational and necessary political programme. He is not obliged to reveal a dogmatic core; he is little inclined to self-clarification or guiding theory; he is not a known, calculable prejudice nor does he seek to set himself up as a *pouvoir neutre* or a *gardien*: to the existing British Constitution his conduct has been consistently destructive. Through his sacramental yet uto-pian political rhetoric, so inappropriate in its terms to the jour-neyman practitioner, he undoubtedly raises cohorts among the excitable and the religiose.

Blair does not officiously claim the status of an intellectual and, as his authority has grown, he seems to have felt less and less need for the illumination, guidance or knowledge that social or political theorists, dead or living, might bring to the 'process' of British regeneration. So far he seems to have relied on what is immediately at hand: his own charged sociability, the play of a romantic imagination, a stock of simple, communicable images, advice, counsel and instruction from various *familiares* at court: in political practice, glosses and tactics from his then Press Secre-tary, Alastair Campbell; in the larger and loftier sociology from Anthony Giddens; in trenchant, practical history from Lord Jenkins. Above all, he relies upon his own sense of what may be done immediately in terms of visibility, performance and there-fore headlines. He visits a hospital at midnight, 'rescues' a tired swimmer and rides a bicycle in triumph through Amsterdam. In this, of course, he differs only in insatiability and alacrity from other leading politicians.

Unmoved by and largely ignorant of history, deriving no strength from the idea of restoration, Blair invokes the lan-guages of regeneration and qualitative change. Yet his executive is not immediately innovative. What he seeks is to carry things through to another but even more conclusive settlement. Eco-nomically and politically, he governs with the grain of what he considers to be the ascendant interests economic and political — the economics usually subsuming the political. The Conserva-tives may be exhausted or 'degenerate' but he fully accepts the market base and general shape of the Thatcher settlement: he is also content to be the beneficiary of Major's balance and prudence after 'Black Wednesday'. In these spheres he is, after all, not a revolutionary but an usurper. In foreign policy he supplements whatever he conceives to be the *force majeure*, invariably the superpower, USA, together with anything that can be mobilized from the 'international community' under the NATO alliance. He is an enthusiast for the punitive power of President Clinton's 'Aerial Board of Control' in Serbia. 'As Easy as ABC', prophesied Kipling in 1912.

Generally, what Blair provided was new wind in the sails. The notable exception was the maintenance by his predecessors of the United Kingdom as a unitary state and their defence of the House of Lords as a more than satisfactory going concern. But even in his proposed expulsion of hereditary peers from the second chamber and devolution of powers to assemblies in Scotland and Wales, in his seeming openness to not easily calculable changes in the structure and strength of the historical political parties that might be effected by electoral reform — and his blithe acceptance of the consequences of British adoption of the European Bill of Rights — Blair, far from being a pathbreaker, is taking up proposals long advanced by the Liberal Democrats and their forerunners. He may be intent upon shaking the foundations but even his constitutional reforms are a kind of usurpation. On the financial and political integration of the European Union and Britain's participation in it, so far he has practised within the same bracket of 'constructive' yet temporizing tactics as employed by Major. But on the outcome he is characteristically prophetic. 'At the end of five years in power I vow that we will have built a new constructive relationship with Europe. This is my covenant with the British people. Judge me upon it.'

At a more earthly level, strategically advised by friends and aides, Blair campaigned to loosen the allegiance of a sizeable segment of the English middle class to the ill-led and unpopular Conservative government. As the politician of consensus and 'good sense', of Christian provenance, who put himself forward as the prospective, modern, enlightened manager of an already prospering economy, Blair was difficult to identify as *hostis*, the public enemy, by comfortable, apolitical, untutored Conservatives — even though, at the Opposition despatch box, he appeared, in his vehemence and derision, unmistakably as *inimicus*, the bitter, personal enemy of John Major, the prosaic, responsible, officeholding St. Sebastian.

With public philosophy plucked loosely from the air, Blair promised high-toned, fame-seeking government, well above the heads, one suspects, of the unillumined, uncivic sectors of the middling orders who so surprisingly voted for him in such large numbers. Seemingly they were as undisturbed by New Labour's open threat to inherited political institutions and culture and to the *patria* itself as were those big corporate, commercial interests who, avowedly 'modern', ruthlessly enterprising and peculiarly Social Darwinian in outlook, turned to New Labour, now the declared party of business, as a new ally in the global struggle for markets. Thus, to use Burkean terms, the moral agency of a great 'movement' or party was subordinated to unmediated political talent in order to achieve, not merely office but also a reversal of ends and purposes.

This protean capability is illustrated at another level. While at the outset he displayed a Gladstonian capacity to move issues into loftier and loftier categories so as to suck familiar earth from under the feet of some of his enthused followers, Blair has had no difficulty at all in keeping up a seemingly unfabricated empathy with the People and in demonstrating a constant bias towards the facile and the democratic. 'I am a modern man. I am part of the rock and roll generation — the Beatles ... colour TV. That is the generation I come from.' Blair chooses to go with the crowd: he owns himself a child of his time without the temerity to discriminate or resist.

He has many intentions and inventions but if he is to exploit such dominance as a liberal democracy affords he must also achieve both consistency and robustness of mind. If he is to make a settlement comparable with that of Thatcher he must surely free himself from those obstructions to rule thrown up by that very liberal democratic pluralism which he claims to foster. He cannot possibly be the slave of the polls and the forums, of mere incoherent opinion. If he is to take up the opportunity opened up to him by his grand electoral triumph, effectively develop a branching *idée directrice*, he must surely adhere to his decision for radical change and carry through 'the meaningful action'. Liberalism must prove too diffuse a guide for Blair. For such an agency, such 'a hand of history', it is the British Parliamentary 'elective dictatorship' that seems to fit like a glove.

For such dominance, dependant on the overwhelming majority of a single party in the Commons, the Labour movement as a whole will, after so many lost years, surely settle. Tired of unfruitful decades of merely 'incremental-adaptive' forms of change will it not make room for the 'supernatural virtue' of this rare leadership. For, despite his nimble, market-square accessibility, the easy route to his Christian name, his strenuous amiability and invasive familiarity, has not Blair already created that space all round himself that is a prescription for domination: space, perhaps not between himself and his reputed duumvir, Alastair Campbell, but certainly between himself and his Cabinet, between himself and Parliament and even between himself and his party? To space he has added the time given to him as 'the statesman of long breath' confidently looking to the General Election beyond the next, seemingly unconstrained by established political system or process.

This then is Blair grounded, engaged in the almost conventional task of exercising commissioned authority as the leader and agent of his party. But there is within another potentiality, the product of another state of mind: the imaginative and creative innovator of unusual political prowess who has emerged from the deep Sunday thinkers, the religiose, discussing classes, with mission rather than commission. In this vein he visualizes a new, unfolding world of politics, discursive, tentative and experimental, not of enemies but friends, a world not of established dominations and powers but unpledged to the existing order of things, indeed, to existing modes of being, and open to change through discussion, consensus, 'constructive engagement' and good counsel. This is Blair, the modern man become statesman, at last consummating the promise of politics of the romantic and ineffectual 1960s.

This is the leader who goes neither exclusively Right nor Left but straight forward, one who, rejecting Britain's past, locates his *patria* in the domain of the future. Indeed he disparages his inheritance; his task is 'to build a new and young country that can lay aside the old prejudices that have dominated our land for generations'. He makes an historic choice for modernity and change that releases him from party, party-system and constitution. He seems to have no setbacks, no hardships, to be unburdened by mere experience, to be, indeed, the very reverse of 'the pilot who weathered the storm', the very image of the 'active-anticipatory' leader called to rather than fashioned for high office. In this role he seems to have only minimal attachments and uncertain anchorage. His words are to inspire rather than bind or loose or even locate. Despite the Third Way there is little indication of where he is going.

This prescribed path to national renewal runs through the centre, taking its direction from the aims and purposes of all existing parties, from both capitalism and socialism, from private and public enterprise, from individual and community, from assent and dissent, from energies both public and voluntary. Between these poised polarities the country will move forward confidently into the future, into modernity. This median stance, this choice of compromise after compromise, reconciliation of contending interests and values, can hardly imply anything more than the universal application (applicable apparently to even Russia and South Africa) of a formal liberalism as a solution for all political problems. It is not an end but a way, absorbing the higher and enlightened, disparaging and dissipating the backward, residual and outdated.

As a state of mind liberalism is appropriate to a numinous master-politician seeking creativity in an unchartable future. For it exudes good will to all others, even enemies, promises habitual cooperation in a new mode of politics. What it sets up is government by discussion without end, without substantial plateau, in which the dialectical, the conversational, forever prevails over the eristical, the contentious. Thus it rejects what Weimar Germans called the party-state, the state divided up among the parties, Parliament as an arena for perpetual tribal conflict. All these are elements in Blair's liberalism as is the, not necessarily complementary, practice of inspirational leadership of the Gladstonian kind, constant display of innovative 'heroic

energy' careless of consequences. This is a vein of passionate liberalism, now forgotten by most Liberals who have, in practice,
become as sobersided and incremental as other politicians and
as content to do the next thing.

Externally, New Labour's insistence upon an 'ethical foreign
policy' and probable acquiescence in the project to deliver the
United Kingdom, spiritually and culturally reborn and
'rebranded' into the civility of a federal European Union are
both of unmistakable liberal provenance. So too the movement
for electoral reform over which Blair hesitates and the devolution of powers to the territorial or 'ethnic' assemblies within the
island at the considerable risk of diminishing coherent authority
in Westminster, setting up recalcitrant provinces on the frontiers
and perhaps ultimately legitimating separatisms and enmities.

It is certain, however, that Blair does not manifest the whole of
the liberal syndrome. It is with illiberal zest that he attacks the
'life situations' of his adversaries in the Commons and with
painstaking and sometimes petty news manipulation deprives
them of publicity. It is with effrontery that he uses his patronage
to win over disaffected leading politicians among the opposition
to his side. He lacks some of 'the supreme generosity' which
Ortega y Gasset attributed to liberals. Before Blair will 'share
existence with the enemy', it seems that they must be suborned
and/or capitulate. He is fundamentally at odds with any
resumption of the alternate rule of two great parties whose complementary periods of office lay at the heart of the efficacy of the
old going concern. Parliament is primarily a place for televisual
acclamation and confrontation. There have been Prime Ministers in this century such as Balfour, Baldwin and Churchill, who
illumined or educated the House of Commons: Blair is not
among them. For discussion or persuasion, dramatic expendi-
ture of spiritual and intellectual energy, he prefers the captive
audience of the political theatre or of the extra-Parliamentary
focus groups rapidly becoming institutionalized.

Under what influences or tutelage was developed this
unusual distaste in a British Prime Minister for the 'tribalism'
and inveteracies of conventional British party politics, in particular, for the solidarities of the Labour Party, must remain largely

a matter of conjecture. So too must the residual core, or prepossessions, if any, of the romantic political actor. Blair's political conduct does not stem from known sedimentations of experience and thought. We cannot predict which state of mind will prevail and which will not — at least not until the entrails have been consulted. Despite his numerous public pledges he seems to have his political being in an indeterminacy from out of which he lights on occasions and opportunities. He cannot, as yet, be condensed into a constant exercise of personified virtue, solidified (like Thatcher) into a calculable political role. He is still mainly intent on performance.

At the outset, it seems that, as a policy-maker, Blair was drawing as freely as was practicable upon such articulate progressivism as then belatedly and fitfully pulsed through the body of British politics. Simply because Britain had been widely categorized as an *ancien régime*, the accent had to be upon a newer and higher order of things. The old framework and repertory of politics were condemned. But because Britain had so long resisted or delayed change, constitutional reform too had acquired its time-tested repertory, resting mainly in the care and advocacy of the Liberal Democrats. Chastened by their long exclusion from office though they might be, Liberals remained in charge of those 'higher things' to which Blair is attracted like a moth to a candle. It is therefore not at all surprising that, for practical guidance, example and instruction, Blair turned to their leaders.

From Ashdown, then Liberal Democrat leader, he has taken indeed much of his constitutional programme — to date his most anti-Conservative policy. From Lord Jenkins, in particular, he learned of a long-thwarted, putative, liberal consensus which, after running in a divided channel in Britain for much of the twentieth century, was now available for tapping by the master-politician at a single electoral point. Thus Blair, at last, found some history that he could use. Through a New Labour-Liberal Democrat *entente* or coalition, the highly active neo-Liberalism of Edwardian England, disrupted by an ancient Lib-Lab quarrel, could now resume its single flow. Upon this course would be borne constitutional and social reform, an ethical foreign policy, sustained participation in international concert, 'national efficiency', purposive national education or rather 'socialization', a 'truce of God' between the political parties, the final settlement of the Irish question, 'home rule all round' and so on.

Well before May 1997, Blair was openly moving on to political ground long occupied by the Liberal Democrats and their forerunners. He owned affinities and agreement with liberal policies but sought not the supplanting of but alliance or 'understanding' with the third party. Thus there were developed two strategies: a lesser and a greater; the one bent on survival and entrenchment; the other on expansion and subsumption to the end of installing a new political order. Both were to be pursued with the aid of Ashdown, intent on gaining Cabinet office and participating fully in a national coalition government. It was this aspiration which was for a time to be strengthened, once Blair was in office, by the co-option of Ashdown and leading Liberal Democrats into a Cabinet Joint Consultative Committee. The first, the minimal, strategy, was devised to maintain in office, by modest coalition or understanding, a New Labour administration which had only bare or minority support in the Commons. This precautionary design was rendered unnecessary by Blair's landslide victory.

The greater, indeed grand, strategy, was aimed at the realignment of British party politics. This entailed the construction of a new centre party, alliance or coalition, representing the widest range of identities and interests; a formation intended to absorb or dominate all formerly freestanding parties. Such is presented as the fruit of Blair's insight into his times: his envisioning of a new polity based on the constructive engagement of all groups and parties, the deprecation of all tribes and frontiers (not contained or sanctioned by devolution). Blair is not to come to power to alternate with an adversary but, seemingly, to carry out a conclusive programme. Like that other notable/notorious, political deviant, Viscount Bolingbroke, in the early eighteenth century, he intimates that his own inclusive party may be the last. For as far as can be seen, dominance will rest upon a new durable, left-of-centre, Europhile establishment.

Operatively, this fundamental shift would mean the supplanting of the formally now ruling, still class-representing
Labour party by a prehensile Labour-Liberal party alliance or
party, individualist yet communitarian, 'ethnic' yet non-tribal,
'patriotic', yet capitulatory (the remote loyalty is to 'Europe'). In
short, 'a standing miracle'. A turn of the imagination, some time
ago among those who now constitute the ruling few, had, in
practice, eventuated in an enterprise to re-structure British party
politics in such a way that the Tories would never hold office
again. 'Old' Labour would sink to constitute an unwitting, inert
sediment at the base of enlightened New Labour. The dwindling
Conservative party would become an isolated English Nationalist rump — the last vestige of an autonomous English/British
patria — its 'one nation' left wing being duly absorbed into the
enlightened hegemony at the centre.

All this remains adumbration rather than project or design.
Before Blair there still lies a choice of modes and styles; between
an 'elective dictatorship' based upon the dominance of a single
party in the Commons, and pivotal government through a
long-lasting, secure coalition successfully holding in balance
right-centre economic policies and left-centre social policies.
The first mode requires assured incumbency — with 'strict and
authoritarian discipline', says Blair — left-of-centre but robust
rule involving regular demonstrations of implacability and,
probably, resumption of fundamental ties with Old Labour. This
is Blair dominant, Blair as 'chief of men', briskly attending to a
kernel of rational and necessary politics well within his mandate, Blair owning his dependence on a single party, Blair emu-
lating Thatcher by achieving an acknowledged settlement.

The second mode will require him to act as a pivot, mediator
or persuader in a grand coalition moving along his Third Way
towards no substantive end but simultaneously effecting a qualitative change in the nature of the conduct of politics itself, thus,
by converting his foes into his friends, denying its essence. Thus
Blair endorses Peguy by turning politics into mysticism. Such a
median orientation dispensing with an unusual, innovative virtue in the leader, obviates the need for a dogmatic core of belief,
for maintaining party solidarity and for consistency of style. At

the same time it may inaugurate a liberalism inimical to clear volition. For there is always the possibility that liberal pluralism, by empowering unbiddable citizens rather than biddable subjects, may run against the grain of rule itself. At the least, it may diminish the autonomy of a leadership already perhaps seriously hampered, as Thatcher's was not, by a mandate for constitutional reconstruction and by an inordinate 'modernism' which precludes New Labour from invoking a notably successful national past.

Nevertheless, it is to the liberal enlightened that Blair promises most. Like the Liberal Democrats and their advance guards, Charter 88 and the think-tank *Demos*, all seeking to institutionalize new and imaginative ways of politics, Blair is at odds with a British Constitution no longer benign, no longer a model for a modern state. At the heart of his political rationalism lies a plot to remodel or transform old political institutions obstructive to his 'project'. In this radical defiance of the conservative order of convenience, this revolutionary move, this demonstration of his belief that by re-structuring political institutions you can change the social, economic and political order for the better, Blair commits himself to incalculable upheaval. He shows himself not to be uninstructed — far from it — but to be uninitiated.

Old Labour accepted and worked through the British Constitution as given. Under its occasionally mystagogic leader New Labour paradoxically would demystify and modernize it. Proposals for reform have therefore followed thick and fast: for executive-expediting change in the Commons; for electoral reform, possibly for proportional representation, as decided by referendum; for legislative and governmental decentralization through devolved assemblies to placate ethnic or regional particularisms within the United Kingdom; for new modes of popular consultation within the electorate at large through focus groups and policy forums to ensure rational discussion of and agreement on serious issues by all men of good will — in fact, agencies of persuasion as well as intelligence; and finally, to the delight both of sixth-form radicals and *les tricoteuses* of the assembly, for the reconstruction of the second chamber of Parliament, disembarrassed at last of its hereditary members. In all these reforms, Blair's commitment both to a 'born-again' nineteenth-century liberalism and to the institution of a truly modern and pluralist liberal democracy is beyond question.

More surprising in a professedly practical Labour politician, necessarily concerned with the sheer obduracy of 'life forms' and the infeasibility of a united, resolved, political community, than Blair's conversion to liberal institutional reforms is Blair's active propagation of high liberal theory. Within coalition, consultative committee, inter-party meeting, policy forum or focus group, his declared aim is to elicit and sustain a progressive dialectic among all participants through rational discourse and critical self-reflection. The end is the reconciliation of all values and claims under a party which purports to be 'the political arm of nothing less than the British people as a whole'. Dissent is there to be processed by reason, by the force of superior argument in open forum. Ideas must lose their resistant capacities, be clarified and synthesized; groups must abjure their hostilities and soften their hard edges — echoes of David Owen and Roy Jenkins — and accommodate themselves in consensus for the greater good. All this liberal 'elevation' from a party which in office has been more adept than any other in our time in projecting and controlling a particular climate of opinion for its own ends.

There is every indication, however, that his public enemies must multiply (personal enemies he has, of course, duly acquired as a result of his ruthless struggle for the leadership within a bemused Labour party). Within the public arena he ceaselessly invokes either transforming values (and necessarily interests) or himself as the embodiment of them and thus finds himself plunged into a plurality of passions. The result of such immersion and consequent depreciation or scouting of the values of others must consist in a diversity of animosities. Liberal democracy creates a tessellation of opinions, fosters, as Santayana noted, 'a reign of unqualified ill-will'. It multiplies and entrenches conflict, produces not merely competitors but also enemies. The inculcation of values through continual edification from above must stimulate counter-values among those discountenanced or dispossessed of worth by the 'unassailable' Leader and his aides.

Blair's unusual preoccupation, as a British Prime Minister, is with the moral transformation of the country. As such, despite, some would say, because of his mirroring of the neo-liberal economic policies of Thatcher, he is profoundly un-Conservative. There is, it has been said, 'no textbook of Conservatism but the history of Britain'. Essentially, Conservative literature has been a commentary on that history, an extraction of perennial values from insular habits and practices. Blair's intention is to conceal or disavow this inherited version of the past. In no sense is he seeking to assimilate Conservatism; he is, in fact, engaged in a *Kulturkampf* against it. Through his undiscriminating patronage and cultivation of an artless 'popular culture' and with it a whole gallery of performers of negligible intrinsic worth, he is deliberately cutting the painter with the best that is known and thought. In a venture such as this, not gratuitously but aforethought for electoral reasons, it may be that Blair is provoking deeper, better informed and more durable resentments than those incurred by his religiose yet utopian politics. To these may be added not only those smouldering in Old Labour and residual Tory but, spreading wider, those harboured in individual, group or movement continuing to stand by the world as it has come to be.

It is, however, through his vaunted political talent rather than through any defining enmities that Blair claims potency either as mandated, programmatic Legislator or as Grand Pivot of a durable Liberal-Labour coalition or something pitched in between these modes of government. As a romantic political actor he must have some difficulty in choosing which way. Which mode will be adopted depends upon what must be done, i.e. enacted. So he awaits his own resolution. Yet it does seem that, with no impediment either in Parliament or in party to his exercise of commissioned prerogative powers and with no real need at all for assistance from any other party or wing or faction thereof, he is most likely to use his authority to the full through the lease of power conventionally afforded to him through his overwhelming party majority in the Commons.

The alternative mode, as chairman of a coalition, would put a premium on forbearance, benignity, moderation and patience. None of these has a notable place among Blair's qualities. In his pursuit of rapid rebuttal or conclusive assertion, whether he is *en plein air*, in swift gratulatory progression through the streets, grave or bright and shining in television or radio studio, he has a penchant for summary *ex cathedra* statements which neither bind nor loose. He rejoices in the Tower of Babel created by the media. He prefers gesticulatory, finger-stabbing indictment to discourse or debate. He has little recourse to 'communicative rationality'.

Cast as moderator or balancer in a grand coalition, Blair would surely be robbed of his dramatic occasions. Would he not be more at ease as a staged polarity, a primed coherence, preferably a dominance, in a field of force, even better as a personification of 'Energy in the Executive' — on, say, the steps of Downing Street or at the Conference podium? He is, after all, deeply engaged in a monodrama. He is the providential 'Single Person', making what Shirley Williams once called 'a quantum jump'. Must he not be aware that, for the achievement of fundamental political change in Britain, only an elective dictatorship is appropriate?

As a romantic liberal, Blair would seem to have his being in an indeterminacy that must inhibit decision. Yet decision and its effective execution is inherent in all government — without them Blair can attain to no style. Romantic activity, it has been maintained by Carl Schmitt, is a contradiction in terms. 'Where political activity begins, romanticism ends.' Already, therefore, Blair's romanticism may be on the wane. Perhaps from the beginning it was no more than a youthful guise, a means of gaining attention. From the outset of his political ascent he was aware of the need for a more realistic stance. Hence, his early recourse to the device of the Calvinist Covenant as proof of his presumptive virtue and dedication to effective political action. Before and through the General Election of 1997 he, the romantic novitiate, offered a Covenant to the British people promising them a new beginning. That compact, in all its temerity, the British people were deemed to have endorsed or sealed by bestowing on Blair that astonishing landslide victory. 'You shall be my People and I will be your Lord.' The only thing that could follow was the deliverance of Blair's people.

This dramatic event may seem to mark no significant departure from romanticism but it is nevertheless a clear and specific pledge of specific action. For Calvinists were far from being romantics: they struck some of the most earnest, indeed grimmest, notes in history. Nor was the device of the Covenant acceptable to liberals for whom the future is open and unfolding rather than determined. It is surely much harder for the Grand Pivot of a liberal coalition to be a Covenanter than for an elective dictator for whom a mandate may easily be translated into a Covenant. As a theological category or a political device in seventeenth-century Scotland, the National Covenant brought not collaboration but conflict, not peace but the sword. Primarily, it stood not just for armed resistance to popes and bishops, heresies and schisms but also for their extirpation. Some historians derive this deep commitment not so much from the Hebrew Covenant as from the practice of Scottish murder bands. The instant loyalty was to the 'public band' raised in defence of a particular community, ethnic or religious or both. It could be used to defend, deny or bind authority. For Blair, it directed and bound authority to specific actions.

In Scotland the Covenant involved the harsh disciplining of the people, constantly demanding what Blair in one of his recent political sermons, called 'backbone not backdown' from both community and party. Unexercised virtue and 'watery fidelity' are, it seems, of no use to New Labour. The Covenant gives Blair what romantic liberalism cannot, a line of march, a mandate. As 'sound bite', it steels him towards the exercise of commissioned executive powers, towards an exacting, binding style. And as possibilities dwindle and prospects fade — as they must — and he has to come to terms with what obdurately persists, this is what he will need to realize what remains from his 'new age of achievement'.

Tony Blair and the Ideal Type

I

This then is Blair in the middle passage from platform intentions to political performance. What has been projected discursively and romantically, intimating another mode of politics seeking lasting accommodations among contending interests and values, the imperatives of parties and nostrums, is crystallizing into specific policies of radical reform: of public finance and public services, of welfare provision; of re-planning the National Health Service by improving throughput, shortening waiting lists, raising standards and so forth; above all, of educational services, of content and methods of teaching in the schools, of reorienting universities away from such educational interludial ends as they might still entertain towards the increase of the nation's contribution to the world's wealth — all to be driven through by central powers and dominions by means of exhortation and reproach: invidious distinctions, 'naming and shaming', goal — and target shaming, comparative statistics, competitive league tables. As yet all this micro-management, micro-gubernation, has by report achieved imperfect or disappointing results, but the energies expended in this vast surveillance of these and other public services testify as no other engagements can to the essentially *executive* nature of the New Labour government. Blair is primarily an executive seeking, above all, to avoid or obviate any resistances to the accomplishment of his comprehensive task. There are no checks to power and will, to 'what Tony wants'.

In other spheres, such as financial services, telecommunications, electricity, gas and the like, the interposition of a comprehensive range of regulatory bodies with penal policing powers as well as shaping social and political ends, in practice lying well beyond and sometimes inimical to the strict needs of the competitive market, reinforces the impression of central drive. Supervening this reshaping of local practice, intention and autonomy are some as yet unevaluated, inchoate, uncompleted or perhaps merely projected constitutional reforms: needless and hazardous 'ethnic' devolutions within the double-island, together with threats of centrally instigated English regionalization to come for which 'the mere inhabitants' have never spoken — all erosive of *British* national identity and sovereignty, and often destructive of established lucidities and orders of convenience, not to speak of time-honoured and time-proved institutions such as the House of Lords — all at the command of what Max Weber would have recognized as independent political leadership in action. It might have been an 'enlightened despot' at work.

For despite the notable partition of political offices and spheres of action in 1994 by the then leading undertakers of a future New Labour government, which concedes the conduct of economic and social policy to Gordon Brown, Blair unequivocally never sees himself as other than the prime mover in British politics. The prerogative power is vested in him alone. The ends, strategies, the intentions of New Labour may often derive from ideas and projects circulating among the conjectured or putative cabal or coven which launches the inner campaign or coup, returns Blair, first, as the conclusive victor on the electoral battlefield, and then sustains him as *vox* and front. But it is as supreme decision-maker, unencumbered by anything so formal as an effective plural executive or even a general staff, taking counsel at will, that Blair dominates and rules. He is the one who casts the die, playing the part he becomes the part. And this role, that of the *tout seul*, near-plebiscitarian ruler, the place-giver, the patronage dispenser, and at the same time, the outsider, subsumes all other roles simply because he is politically empowered by *demos*: all of a sudden, Blair is projected into the world of idea, will and decision — out of a liberal indeterminacy. It is not necessarily a world of checks and balances and Parliamentary democracy. His role is to pit executive power against 'most certain enmities' at home and abroad. Amity and cooperation are not enough.

Decision not only gives direction and form to his insular regime and its fate in a wider world but also breaks down almost preternaturally into personal intensive management of public services and enterprises through an ever-expanding bureaucracy. These untiring exertions of supervening political power, this self-gratulatory managerial passion for measuring and publicising the results hot-foot as they appear is best instanced by the sedulous, increasing surveillance of the Treasury of Gordon Brown, Blair's satrap, partner and rival, through his 'public service agreements' with Whitehall departments. Everywhere there are goals to be reached, quotas to be met, statistics to be recorded, hurdles to be cleared.

Blair's reform of the public services is a personal exercise of the omnicompetent will. He assumes enthusiasm, the urgency and the practical bent of Peter the Great as apprentice carpenter in the shipyards of Deptford. Yet he is capable of overriding the stored experience of classroom, shop-floor, ward and yard in the name of the exemplary, the renovatory, the modern, the better practice. The task forces of bureaucracy will see that rationalized rearrangement and redisposition prevail. Inspection, review, overview, regulation keep everyone in the great taskmaster's eye. Thus the old country, too long content with being rather than becoming, is to be converted into a modern, model going concern. The immediate end is not only to be knowledgeable, literate and skilled in the modern way, particularly in the 'knowledge economy', but *also* to create a nation in which — echoing Macmillan — the end is to be rich. The values which lie behind this earnest overhaul do not provide the imperatives upon which a modern *patria* may come into being. But the end of the diffuse exhortation, *enrichissez-vous*, is nevertheless clearly political, i.e. an engagement in struggle and volition to achieve a meaning and a goal rooted, for the moment, in the subjectivity of the prime mover. The major 'right decisions' are yet to flow from harboured intentions. The mobilization of renovated insular power, whether for universal or particular ends, is, as yet only a matter for surmise.

Blair is engaged in 'mighty acts'. Like God, he is engaged in continuous creation or recreation; like God, he needs ceaseless strenuous personal projection as single initiator or instigator, as single master-builder, executive and legislator. The people may have sovereignty and indeed empower but he alone is in a position to decide. Blair therefore must be something more than 'a public *smiling* man', a progenitive father who goes on exotic holidays, is invariably charming, empathetic and sympathetic. What he has to seek through his hyperactivity, his omnipresence, is a kind of transcendence and omnipotence, a sentient democratic identity in culture and spirit of ruler with ruled that his predecessors have long lost. Blair is therefore intensely interested in how the media assess him. He tells his *familiares*, the pollsters and advisers of his inner circle, that he wishes to pass 'as a man driven by strong beliefs'; as a ruler 'standing up for Britain'; to be personally associated with 'immediate action … something tough, with immediate bite', as well as with 'touchstone issues'. The ambiguities of his egregious churchmanship, Anglican and Roman Catholic, as well as his professed pursuit of the highest liberal values in secular politics, both domestic and foreign, his undaunted search for affinities with emerging foreign statesmen, even those untoward in record, mien and stance — for Blair 'the new', *ipso facto*, acquires a kind of virtue — all contribute to his acceptance as a serious, catholic, inclusive, *'omnium gatherum'* diplomatist of Third Way provenance for whom no head of state is in schism or beyond the pale. Nor anyone with a private army. Here we have a kind of beneficence or capacity for undiscriminating trust quixotically exhibited. Even the *Daily Telegraph*, while conceding that Blair is profoundly un-Conservative in that he sees no value in national independence and considers that patriotism is 'closely related to racism and xenophobia', judges him 'an able man with a serious purpose'.

Blair is, however, something more than an 'intent', resolved statesman, a rational, moral agent in an irrational world. He is also a covenanted ruler. When he strikes out at home and abroad into the chaotic plurality of contending interests and values, some merely perverse and conservative, some dark and diabolical, he does so, in all singularity, as one particularly charged to fulfil God's purposes and, sometimes, congruently, his own, once and for all. The people await the delivery of Blair's promise of renewal or transformation of human relationships in Britain under New Labour. Indeed, when Blair is overwhelmingly elected to office on 1 May 1997, the nation, according to the Archbishop of York, is declared to have spoken for the rehabilitation of faith and trust in the political life of the island. Expectations are now high for a better Britain. The British people have made a covenant with New Labour. This covenant is 'the formation upon which all right relationships are built', going beyond mere contract for defined and limited purposes. Trust has been sought and given and, were this trust to be fractured, the basis of confidence in democracy itself would be undermined. 'The thunderings and lightnings of Sinai are a timely reminder to us all — both of grace and judgement.' Thus is Blair's secularized charisma returned to sanctity to be refurbished in grace. The Conservatives must not spoil all this by descending 'into a morass of recrimination and party strife'. For as the Rev. Peter Thomson, Blair's mentor on Christian Socialism, insists: 'something happened yesterday. People said we needed a fresh start. They said 'No' to the polarizations of the past.'

The imperative values of the Covenant not only propel Blair into the undedicated, disordered life of the nation; they also thrust him into the wider world where ultimately as a 'unifier' he hopes to play a part in establishing 'a new global consensus' analogous to the agreement among political parties to be reached domestically. Immediately, in Kosovo, Sierra Leone, Afghanistan and Iraq, he pursues an 'ethical foreign policy', gives dynamic leadership to progressive, liberal wars — particularly through *vox* — and foretells further 'mighty acts'. He sides with the big battalions of 'a great and powerful friend' who, through his near-monopoly of available public force, has the capacity to preserve or restore the global order. He senses the necessity of quick, conclusive victories; he confirms 'the most important alliance in history: the special relationship with the USA' in order to collaborate in the conduct of a punitive 'just war' against a Mesopotamian tyrant identified by President Bush as the leading member of a demonized 'evil axis', as the indubitable *foe*.

The concepts of the 'just war' and the 'just cause', insisting that those against whom war is to be waged are getting no more than their deserts, have their provenance in the attempts of the Early Fathers of the Church to reconcile militarism and the shedding of blood with the necessity of performance of duty by Roman Christian soldiers for whom killing of any kind was against Christian teaching. These ideas prevailed throughout the Middle Ages but, from the seventeenth century, were replaced by the concept of the 'just enemy' — with the aim of limiting and humanizing the conduct of warfare in the field. Since then, however, the concept of the 'just war' has periodically been revived — notably in the twentieth-century World Wars in which the protracted intensity of the dissociation and enmity of the contending powers rendered the idea of a 'just enemy' inapposite. For Liberals, in particular, the First World War becomes, according to Irene Cooper Willis, a 'Holy War' with 'idealism harnessed to the war chariot'. War takes on 'the lineaments of an ideal combat' against the satanic splendour of valour and militarism: it becomes 'a war to end war' and establish a new order. In both World Wars *justa causa* returns. Both these 'hyperbolic' conflicts are converted into just wars against their supposed and demonized instigators. No longer categorized as 'just' but as 'absolute', the enemy is now the satanic *foe*, the devil incarnate in a liberal Holy War.

In our time just wars are waged by those nations still 'struggling to be free', for or against Communists and Fascists, against partisans and 'terrorists'. The state may be involved but the conflict is not necessarily between states alone. 'Just wars' may well be congruent with 'total wars' and compatible with 'total enmity'. Primarily, the *justa causa* is identified by theologians, pronounced by secular moralists who do not acknowledge 'the rod of God', by religiose heads of government or state who seek to add moral sheen to political intention, by exhilarated liberals intent on universalizing and rendering absolute or imperative their personal values. It is just the slogan for those who pursue 'global intervention', like Woodrow Wilson, Bush and Blair. It represents the triumph of *jus internum* over the *jus externum*, of conscience over political circumstances or the way of the world. It seeks the triumph of Weber's ultimate ends. No price is too high for this.

To the enlightened and ardent Blair, avowedly pursuing an 'ethical foreign policy' in order to secure a re-ordering of the world in the light of a global consensus, the 'just war' as a means of international morality and justice, as the guarantor of liberal democracy and human rights, has considerable appeal. For the victor of a 'just war' may impose 'war guilt' upon a defeated enemy, exact retribution from him and enforce his recognition of and obedience to the right values and, of course, demand 're-gime change'. So much the Iraq war proves. Saddam Hussein becomes the absolute enemy not only of the enlightened West but also of his own people, the arch-violator of their human rights. Whatever Blair envisages, Saddam becomes the 'irre-deemable' villain, the irreconcilable foe — the archaic enemy, the attack-point for a mobilized Anglo-American liberalism. So do invading armies become the instruments of theologians, preachers, moralists of liberal democracy and impassioned democratic leaders engaged in independent action.

For the eirenic Blair, notably 'no man's enemy, forgiving all'; former believer in unilateral disarmament and member of CND; in domestic politics highly critical of inveterate enmities among historical British parties; the searcher for truth and reconcilia-tion to the point of humiliation or vulnerability with such indu-bitable foes as Adams, Assad and Gadhafi, full passionate engagement in a 'just war' cannot be other than a surprising enterprise. Blair is said to be ungrounded in history but from Kosovo onwards he finds himself fighting necessarily punitive campaigns against iniquitous rulers on behalf of God and humanity, conducting the same kind of Holy War as that embraced by Robert and Roger Guiscard and their Norman armies on behalf of the Papacy in eleventh-century Italy, as that waged by the crusaders against Islam in the Holy Land, and that by confessional states in sixteenth- and seventeenth-century Europe against each other. Blair proves that even without conse-crated banners Godly wars can be waged. He earns his place in the House of Mars.

II

What is the recurring moment for this unusual talent, this startling renovator? It would seem plausibly that it all begins in 'the right decision' for punitive action, involving military intervention, against certain demonized public actors on the stage of the world, each of whom is clearly identifiable to the sentient, liberal or religiose mind as Apollyon ' the utter destroyer or king of Hell'. In Slobodan Milosevic, Osama Bin Laden and, belatedly, and possibly mistakenly, Saddam Hussein, Blair lights upon adversaries, powers of dark-ness, providing both provocations to and occasions for attack and redress in service of the highest values. These moral and military responses to Apollyon mark the emergence of Blair out of the indeterminacies of liberalism, either resolutely as a decisionist fully to embrace the political world of friends and enemies or speculatively or discursively as a romantic bent on creating his own reality, exploring the possibilities of his own subjectivity in which he remains absorbed.

As decisionist, Blair, as the source of imperatives — 'what matters is what Tony wants' — the unresting, perhaps 'ideal type', Legislator and Executive is fully taken up, like God, in a process of continuous creation. For the model is monotheist not polytheist and certainly not pantheist. As such he is unitary, both transcendent and immanent and virtually infallible. As the near-plebiscitary commissioned dictator he develops illiberal preferences. He doubts the truth-finding capacity of parliamen-tary democracy and finds an edge to cut through discussion, debate and negotiation; he eludes or destroys constitutional checks and balances; he discovers a monarchical talent to domi-nate and provides an alternative, as single person, personal ruler, to the conflict of value-laden imperatives. He is undaunted by 'the labyrinth of history'. Within the decisionist, the democrat affirmed by *demos* triumphs over the liberal. So resolved, he quits the Big Tent, contents himself domestically with control by prowess and 'spin' the conflicts of an antagonistic pluralism; but within 'the state of nature' of international politics, pursues humanitarian wars in a last liberal flourish.

> Within my soul there doth conduce a fight
> Of this strange nature, that a thing inseparate
> Divides more wider than the sky and earth ...

Like a deity or a monarch the romantic Blair chooses his 'occasion' for intervention, translation to a higher sphere, departure from reality so as to explore another mode of being or authority; he does this at will from on high. Reality is modified to meet the needs of the actor. His uncommitted ego retains its protean capacities. The romantic remains in a world of possibilities, living, according to Novalis, 'on the froth of better times to come'. Neither causation — nor sudden illumination — are necessarily traceable. What matters is the opportunity. Romantic, autonomous ventures or acts may accompany fateful decisions in the real world of actualities and commitments. 'Going to the wars' implies layers of meaning. Blair endorses Bush's maxim that 'those who are not with us are against us' in the huge, 'shoulder to shoulder' but ragged task of eliminating 'terrorism' from the face of the earth. Thus are the political polarities of what may be an age identified.

Through the alacrity of his support of the provoked American power, as the proponent, mobilizer and untiring coadjutant of what is to become, at core, recourse by 'a coalition of the willing' to humanitarian *just* warfare against what is perceived as rampant tyranny — an ambitious, seemingly endless, quintessentially liberal engagement outside the remit of the United Nations — Blair demonstrates highly visible prowess and élan. His widespread acceptance as an assiduous and highly mobile world statesman and even as a kind of late-developing 'war-lord' is a reward for personality, talent, *vox*, suasion and hyperactivity. In his early days his ready charm and seemingly innocuous amiability earns him the nickname 'Bambi'; his revelatory devotion to humanitarian and liberal causes is not foreseen. His sense of 'the hand of history' on his shoulder at work during the exigencies of reaching a settlement in Northern Ireland is no intimation of the shoulder-to-shoulder commitment, post Kosovo, post '9/11', to the conduct of punitive yet essentially liberal warfare in the name of 'community' against the iniquitous or incompetent dominations in tyrannous or 'failed' states.

No one thinks, early on, that Blair's value-derived imperatives will be consummated in 'blood and iron' on European and Asian battlefields; in precocious, helter-skelter world statesmanship at summit after summit; in vistas of personal eligibility for political primacy such as presidential leadership or equivalent eminence of some kind in an integrating Europe; or even in some 'Atlantic' pivotal office mediating between the two great preponderances of the West (always two): the emerging hegemony of Europe and that already established by the assertive unipolar power of the United States where in ruling circles admiration for Blair is just this side of idolatry. Thus will a British Prime Minister take part in the shaping of what has been called the *'nomos'* of the earth. Assessing his aspirations and conduct on a somewhat lower scale the *Daily Telegraph* concedes that 'The fair-minded person watching Mr Blair would claim that we have a prime minister fit to lead us into war'. Yet Blair speaks not as a British patriot but as a putative leader of a global alliance as well as a voice or agent of a world spirit, both secular and spiritual, a neo-Gladstone going to the wars, a brooder on 'the right decision' on the stage of the world.

III

How and where then do we place Tony Blair, the political virtuoso? What are the touchstones, what, as they say, is the template? Clearly Blair has so far outsoared the British political leadership that we may have to turn away from that distinguished but exclusive tradition to some other measure or matrix, even political science, more likely to be receptive to or inclusive of Blair in all his peculiarity, in Blair as anomaly. For Blair as political performer seems to have no lineage. British politicians characteristically do have roots in the past through birth, class, territory, ethnicity or 'internal' nation, through sensibility, intellectual or religious milieu, deliberate affiliation, through the apperception of the country's understanding of itself.

There is an ancestral gallery rather than a typology of English leading politicians. They operate within particular conventions and tread well-beaten paths to office. There are affinities of temperament and one politician easily catches the voice and adopts the stance of another. The critic or historian can sense both empathies and sympathies, can trace linear continuities over time, evaluate conduct, assess prowess in peace or war, in even tenor or crisis, in achievement or defeat, within what has generally been 'a tradition of confidence' within an institutional matrix forever adjusting but remaining the same. Whatever the processes of election or selection within the parliamentary parties it can be said that the chosen leader characteristically 'emerges' within a knowledgeable party circle well endowed with 'physiognomic tact' and confidently drawing upon cumulative, experienced apperceptions of character, style and current form.

By misfortune or design, Blair does not seem to 'emerge'. There is no slow shaping or lengthy evaluation. He surmounts no ramparts of experienced opinion. Rather he is discovered by scouts and talent-spotters as the new vibrant leader, untested, unnoticed, out of despair and defeats: the chosen agent of renewal, the master-builder of a modern European state, whatever that is, out of one that is old and effete. He is without historical self-understanding or affinities and, as far as is known, has no significant historical reading. Plainly, he is as far in cultural grounding and sense of the past and *patria* as he can be from that other seemingly anomalous Prime Minister, Benjamin Disraeli, who writes his own polemical but perceptive version of English history in order to lay the foundation for his own distinctive political perspective. For Blair history is not productive of any useful polemics; rather, for him, it constitutes the irrelevant and obstructive 'past'; the domain for an undiscriminating nostalgia. The source of outmoded traditions and, in particular and diametrically, of those 'dark conservative forces' so persistently hostile of the re-invention of the world by a ruler who is both romantic *and* rationalist.

It is therefore inappropriate to canonize Blair within an established British linear continuity in time. Rather, I choose to have recourse to a notably resourceful and illuminating segment of political science, to assess or evaluate him within a proven and particularly perceptive typology of political leadership in general within a democracy. For, at first sight, Blair seems a fortuitous approximation — the prime mover is no 'sedulous ape' — of Max Weber's 'ideal type' of independent political leadership in action. Fittingly, he crops up on that British political seed-bed, nursery and training ground that Weber so admires and envies, as one who strives for and obtains, with ends and aims both idealistic and egoistic, power for power's sake in the British House of Commons.

The proposal then is not to evaluate Blair within a canon of other leading politicians within a tradition but to compare him with a sociological 'construction' or hypothesis. The 'ideal type' has been called a methodological device for 'mastering complexity' by setting up a model of expected typicality within a range of regular, meaningful, human action — conduct rather than simple, 'reactive behaviour' — of any individual or social entity: in this instance, of any kind of bearing or exercise of legitimate authority, rule or dominance within a modern democratic state. What is sought is not specificity but generality, a conceptually clarified typicality in what becomes a realm of 'best-practice': of an exemplar, a model, an effective, persisting coherence, elicited from reality, history, anthropology, indeed from whatever is relevant, from worlds not to come but past and present but, in fact, never realized. It is available, among many uses, as a gauge for a particular individual actor within a kind or variety: as a standard or comparison for actual characters, dispositions, humours or dominations in the realm of politics. Weber himself used ideal types 'in order to give meaning and coherence to the otherwise chaotic flux of history'.

IV

As his prototype politician Weber favours a monocrat; thus can effectiveness be assured. The image is Cromwell's Single Person: the strong individual in the strong state. He is evaluated and selected by a knowledgeable elite. Tenor, purport, conduct are necessarily autocratic; he is the victor on the electoral battlefield: the autonomous 'able statesman' at the apex of the political order providing the comprehensive leadership of a Gladstone or Lloyd George. Through him is made available that qualitative statesmanship, sagacious, robust or demagogic as circumstances may demand. In particular, it falls to him to master the egotisms at odds within the party state and dominating the legislature. For Weber, in particular, there must fall to the prototypical monocrat the duty to subordinate the ascending and expanding higher bureaucracy, primarily concerned with decision-making and the execution and administration of public policies, to the necessarily partisan but responsible stratum of political incumbents or placeholders. Through the single prime mover and his close ministerial associates there will develop a governing elite that will sense, interpret and serve the life and destiny of the nation. Policy stems from or is endorsed by the free decision of the inner-determined, value-driven, subjective leader. There is no overarching moral framework — Weber maintains that religion turns men away from the world. His 'ideal type' is not covenanted. There is no salvation to be found in politics which is indeed the arena of 'diabolical powers'.

Blair's authority is not shared. It is true that Gordon Brown as Chancellor of the Exchequer is the unchallenged lord of the ceded territories of social and economic policy and administration and may be seen as a Second Consul with a claim to succeed the first. Another *de facto* political duality — for long operating somewhat surreptitiously without formal acknowledgement, while at the same time persistently remarked as a huge invasion of Blair's singularity and prepotency — lay in what was said to be the often determining influence exerted through the office of the unelected, upstart Alistair Campbell, Director of Communications. For here was, both attestedly and presumptively, a hidden eminence, sedulously and comprehensively acting as 'intelligencer', prompter or instigator, exculpater by denial or rebuttal of the single incumbent and his ministry, the confounder of his enemies public and private; indeed, his voice and his right arm: Bosola to his Duke Ferdinand, Father Joseph to his

Richelieu, Ehrlichman to his President Nixon. But neither of these intimations of dualism has proved a serious threat to Blair's singularity as an 'independent democratic political leader in action'.

Weber's ideal monocrat harbours a dogmatic core of ideas to which he adheres; he approximates to what in our time has been called ' a conviction politician'. It cannot, however, be said that the chameleonic Blair is characterised by the certitude or persistence of his political ideas. He is indeed known for the speed with which he universalises his personal values and moral judgments and applies them terrestrially. Hence the facility of his active moral interventions in this unintelligible world. From these *démanches* one deduces the emancipation of Blair the decisionist statesman from the liberalism and romanticism on which he is nurtured politically but their impress is far from erased. For what characterizes him at least as much as his propellant imperatives is his recurrent indeterminacy; he takes his time actualizing his moment, seizing his day. Sometimes he seems like God himself to be assuming a leisured omnipotence waiting for his 'occasion' or opportunity for casting his die. For the immediacy, the astonishing alacrity of his support for Bush is not characteristic: whether on the British adoption of European currency or the ratification of a European constitution he bides his time. What may seem to need a clear statement of principle or intentions may earn only an equivocal or pragmatic response. Characteristically he does not plunge into the deed. A romantic 'turn of the imagination' may not always conclude in the revelation of a new point of departure. He need not commit himself. The *'occasio'* may not become an exacting, exorbitant cause. In the end he recognizes the *de facto* and is content to be an ancillary. This acceptance of the primacy of reality is residually Weberian.

Blair, it seems, has little regard for discrete and firm political ideas or beliefs, for durable time-honoured and idea-bearing political parties adhering to traditional policies and nostrums. Indeed, he operates by fusing opposing ideas and entertains projects for compromising with and absorbing kindred parties with more policies than political prospects. Thus he extends New Labour's base within the political community while, at the same time, through his Third Way, invoking a multiplicity of contending but alternately reconcilable values, even impera- tives and therefore energies within the polity. So, in Blair's frictionless utopia certain fructifying or progenitive words with calculable potencies are released to mobilize autonomous aspira- tions or objectives for the common good in communitarian felic- ity. These disparate values and policies are assembled, focussed and blended and then set fair not merely to avert discord and col- lision of imperatives but to achieve a new concurrence.

This, to quote Shirley Williams on another 'transformation' of politics, involves 'a quantum jump' to a higher order. Politics from now on is to be about reallocation and re-adjustment of val- ues. Dialectic is to be pressed only to the point of animated mod- eration. Primordial political loyalties are to be dissolved or pushed to the edges of the system — extruded by the extruding centre ceaselessly seeking, under an 'enlightened despot' com- patibilities of motivations. Dominance is to pass to a kind of con- structive liberalism set on instituting not so much a *patria* as an ethical entity of earnestly co-operating citizens. In truth, the world of values is a world of enemies personal and public (*inimici* and *hostes*), in which virtuous wars may have to be fought so that the highest values in the hierarchy may win. Overladen with fantasies becoming values the romantic is likely to take up arms for an illumined truth. But the world as it is offers no conciliation, no consensus, 'no poultice for that sore' even to a *bien-pensant*, all-accommodating 'talent' such as Blair's. Weber himself deprecates romanticism and 'sterile excitation'; he opts for Bismarckian realism. He is deeply involved in the fate of the nation-state and *patria* in a way that Blair is not.

Weber 's 'ideal type' too seeks coherence in a disordered world of values in conflict to which there is no solution except by force or politics. Reason seeks conciliation in vain. Values pro- voke other values and harden into presuppositions and preju- dices, indeed into 'points of attack'. Irreconcilable attitudes to or interpretations of life culminate in a pluriverse of strong states or dominations establishing their own 'meanings' and commit- ments. In sociology Weber is famous for his 'value neutrality' but not in his politics. Ideals are formed and shaped in conflict with other ideals and create their own resistances and tyrannies; principled actions, based on the universalization of locally esteemed evaluations, merits and intrinsic virtues or superiorities, may well disrupt relations and promote conflict within the pluriverse. In Weber there is no grand theory, no global solution: only the positive recommendation to sustain a harmony of strong states and the strong leadership of effective and responsible 'plebiscitarian' statesman, representing and recognizing within the pluriverse assured dominations reflecting the facts of power.

V

The political calling of Weber's active leader demands that there are times when he can do no other than make a stand in his striving for power or for an ideal and that he be strenuously passionate, elementally and psychically engaged in the pursuit of causes. Politics without commitment to ends or beliefs is not possible. Passion is a culminating state of mind, a fusing of wrath and zeal in a stable but vehement subjectivity propelling decisions in a tumultuous pluriverse of values, perhaps charismatically graced or charged but, at the same time, objectively and responsibly channelled. It stems from perspective and will and is fed by the flame of pure intention. It is inescapably partisan. It seeks through conveyance of, the authenticity of and urgent need for recognition of a public policy or purpose to evoke a popular response from a plastic audience, thus to give 'form' selectively to 'the people' by closing a relationship of common assertion, indeed by achieving a kind of conversion, while apotheosing the impassioned performer on stage, platform or screen. In this way judgment, without reservation for affirmed values and imperatives, is taken into the heart of the political debate. At the same time the attendant 'ethic of responsibility' insists that there are constraints upon both self-clarification and commitment. Consequences may not be left to the gods. A prevailing realism ensures that ultimate ends are not in fact pursued. There are limitations upon exemplary decisive performance.

As smiling yet impassioned public man, as inimitable single performer, Blair is more than familiar to us as the central focus of our politics. Whether at party conferences invoking futurity, his favoured realm, in all its promise, eulogizing Britain as the potential model state of the coming century, defining and indicting 'the forces of conservatism', or taking up arms against the 'evil political axis', ethnic oppression and 'terrorism' as such, Blair takes off into messianic promise, dreams and fantasy and transforms the First Lord of the Treasury into a world spirit. Yet he has passion to spare for domestic matters too: fervently to denounce 'trade union wreckers', bitterly to reproach the change — resisting public services for the 'scars' they have inflicted on him, weekly, to indulge in rodomontades, standardized but still foam-flecked, against the guilty, unatonable record of the Conservative Opposition long out of office.

This is far from what Mandeville described as 'skilful management by dextrous politicians', even further from when in office merely 'doing the next thing' which contented a whole race of aristocratic British politicians; it is a deliberate harnessing of the passions. This mode eschews the dispassion of the impersonal statesmanship of the realm whether monarchical or republican. The intent is to excite, to move and transform. This is not a modest attempt to add modifications and increments to the policies of departed 'able statesmen' in a succession of similar political incumbents, each proceeding step by step 'in fruitful party alternation'. According to Sir Ernest Barker:

> Each statesman must plan his work for the life he can reasonably expect; and each must plan it on the assumption that he is likely to be succeeded by a statesman of a different type and party.

Barker's British statesman is 'heuristic' or 'seeking'; he tries to discern the direction in which his countrymen are moving; he has no general line, he proceeds not by application of rationalism but by prescience and discernment. But Blair is no mere steersman. He is the fabricated rather than the crafted leader who does not find himself but is placed *tout seul* at the centre of political action to re-fashion the order in which he has become not at all fortuitously 'the effective focus of the multitude'.

Blair often owns his impassionment by or through cause and enterprise. Yet at the same time his predilection for a romantic self-dramatization means that both convictions and passions may change with states of mind, with the demands of the political narrative in which he finds himself. As an actor he moves with ease from role to role to reflect the inconsistency of his political persona. To this end he has become versed in histrionics which faithfully reflect those responses appropriate to his essentially political meanings and intentions. He invests heavily in 'the politics of intimacy' through which the politician seeks to reveal the authentic, sentient self to be known and trusted. Political discourse is thus focussed not upon measures and policies but upon men, not any objective character or style to which they have attained, but upon their motivations and feelings, indeed their psyches. A politician gains in credibility, stimulates empathy in others because he can re-enact what has moved him personally. Thus he charges himself with a more persistent and persuasive 'secular charisma'. So he spins and casts a spell; he convinces and binds.

These intimacies are not involuntary. 'Art is man's nature.' Continuously practised by body and voice in political intercourse they cannot but become artifices or skills. It is as though, writes Richard Sennett, the affairs of the public domain have become tiresome or hackneyed and it is discovered that any self-revelation will through emotional excitation, sign of grace, empathy, being moved or aroused, being 'touched', will restore import or significance to political communication. Once the contained, inexpressive civil mask that makes an even tenor of existence possible to citizens in a *res publica* is lifted, the politician is assured of reaching and making contact with his audience. What can be more enlivening, more arresting, than the platform performer's exposure of feelings and motivations involved in his staged but essential identification of friends and enemies, his inculpations and exonerations, his illumination of issues and exploration of futures?

According to Sennett, the danger is that the sentient, expressive politician in freely unburdening himself of the decent constraints of tacit civil association may, indeed, reveal all too much of what is unacceptable about himself. It is possible that he may be guilty of incivility in thus burdening those followers who find him intrusive or embarrassing. They may find him either beyond explanation or just too explicable. By vocation the politician traffics in intentions open and covert pursued with ingenuity, imagination and charm. All too easily may his hearers perceive a gulf between appearance and reality — at its simplest, see that 'A man may smile and smile and be a villain'. In short, close relations between leader and followers may expose too much about his self, 'soft' or 'hard'.

Blair is notably at ease in the theatre of politics as one who finds it necessary 'to put [his] heart upon the stage as though it were ill at ease with [him]'. Such, according to Rousseau, is at odds with the pursuit of true human values. An integral part of ourselves is displaced and exhibited histrionically in detachment from 'our natural being' and becomes a contrived effect or counter in a public spectacle or discourse. It has no authentic relation with either actor or audience who are affected only superficially by what is enacted. Always there is a suspicion that an appearance has been substituted for a reality, that a deception has been practised.

> For I will wear my heart upon my sleeve
> For daws to peck at: I am not what I am

It is in the expression of feeling for a cause rather in intimation of sympathy, fellow humanity or regret that the Weberian 'methodological device' and historical figure have most in common. Both are highly subjective, both contend in a world of inimical values. Both take a stand, Weber's conceptual typicality moved by historical exemplars like Martin Luther or Bismarck, Blair, the liberal venturer, the romantic occasionalist, notably but not untypically, by a fateful movement of conjunction, moral and military, with the seemingly irresistible unipolar potency of the USA. Each of the impassioned leaders, the one hypothesized, the other *in media res* has to come to terms with ultimate ends as well as 'blood and iron'. Each subscribes to conviction politics and is driven by his own *daemon*. Each hopes to be sensed as a national leader realizing, through his vision and skills, substantial ends. But if we choose, as well we may, to attribute to what is, after all, put forward as an 'ideal type' from a German source, the known cultural convictions and attitudes characteristic of its creator and so animate the hypothesis with mind, spirit and presence, the abstract and the living exemplars must surely diverge.

Blair cultivates closeness, intimacy and charm in his practice of politics. The public man is under constant private occupation. This amiability and accessibility is however fully compatible with a highly directive liberal imagination in control of an active political rationalism set in motion to realise human desires and dreams, to effect, if necessary, a politics of transformation or destruction, to cast aside traditional attitudes and institutions, to enable the leader to assume, as prime mover, a stance of prescience and virtue within a new essentially liberal moral order, 'a beacon to the world'. This would seem to be the meaning of Blair's headlong political course in pursuit of dreams, bereft of ideology, precise agenda or controls, indeed proceeding intuitively or pragmatically, perhaps romantically, out of liberal indeterminacy. In the end, Blair exploring his 'matrix of possibilities' ends as he must as one who embraces the politics of friend and enemy, as an apostate from liberalism, as a highminded, passionate decisionist.

Yet not for Blair the impersonal control of the 'able statesman' the unmoved, senatorial presence and profile, the steady 'measuring eye' of men and affairs, the schooled *gravitas* before events, contrived or uncontrived, the calm acceptance of the *de facto* deed without revelation of inner feelings. For Blair the teller becomes the tale and his sentience or sensibility suffuses the action. Putting on the agony is indeed complementary to his righteousness. When he makes his decision to mobilize Britain for Bush in the President's war for ultimate ends against Saddam Hussein, he uses his personal and prerogative powers to exact a formal unity from a divided Parliament and people. Behind his Weberian independent action, Blair finds it enough to assert that 'I have never had any doubt that this is the right thing to do'. Like Charles James Fox who has something of the same talent and charm — 'never was anyone more agreeable' — and something of the same ready 'tenderness' — 'nothing more than the vibration of a nerve' — Blair depends upon his feelings for his ethical side. He concurs with Fox's reassurance of himself upon his own rectitude. 'It does not signify as long as one is satisfied that one is doing right'. And, according to Junius, he does this without having a heart.

VI

No conclusive empirical analysis is available to confirm or confute Blair on his solitary moral eminence perilously asserting and launching his *justa causa*. For he is not merely seeking a harmonisation or a restoration of a lost coherence. The end is certain, indeed drastic, political change in another country of which he knows little. Any judgment he makes derives from the application of generalities, necessarily abstract, to changing circumstances and potentialities. Moreover, it is a personal conscience that insists that he can do no other. This is for earnest:

Action is transitory, a step, a blow,
The motion of a muscle — this way or that —
'Tis done, and in the after-vacancy
We wonder at ourselves like men betrayed.

This is a time for resolution of the serried moral criteria, for evaluation of the ripeness of the occasion. Perspective is mobilized and judgment made not in a receding but in a gathering light. In the end the decision is a leap from what Wordsworth calls 'the after-vacancy' into assumption of the burden of what comes to pass, not merely of an outcome but of an *eventus* which Blair is in league to bring about. The load, the apprehension, is replaced by absorption in the execution of independent action in a widening theatre, a sense of value-laden prowess and residual satisfaction in self-preservation as active representative and ruler.

According to Weber such decision-making enters into 'the psychic being' and fate of the nation. It involves pitting in passion the values of the dominant Single Person against such inimical forces as still maintain their resistances at court or in discourse at the highest level, together with the enlisting of such concurring popular lucidities as may adventitiously or extrinsically emerge at all levels of assimilable opinion. From a hierarchy of jostling values, cohorts of support, inchoate and committed, are indiscriminately mobilized in favour of a dominant passion. A kind of vehemence makes its mark on current affairs. Such ingathering, fusing and harnessing of active opinions in favour of a just war, cause or enterprise are fully within the compass of the calling of a leading politician in a mass democracy. They bring the imperatives of his inner determination to an 'attack point'. The measuring eye reaches a judgment appropriate to the highest representative political office. Thus does a Hobbesian 'violence of mind', the pumped up public utterance of a venturing political ego, with design and intention, seek in public space echoes, applause and 'glory'.

For Weber, notably, the rightness of the decision depends upon the bringing into balance or fusion of two ethics: the ethic of ultimate ends and that of personal responsibility. The values of the believer as embodied in *causa*, extremity or exigency may be ultimate but they cannot be inflexible. They must, in practice, be modified by means or circumstances. A 'right' political decision cannot escape from political criteria: absolute ends must yield to actualities that change the frame of action, confound the predictable. The closed mind that, according to de Jouvenel, alone secures success in the field, may be prised wide open. Facts and imperatives may have to yield to other facts and imperatives. Blair's 'right decision' is an unmediated declaration, as it stands, for ultimate ends. Conscience is sovereign; action stems from a leap of faith. The stand, *in extremis*, in pursuit of virtue either recks not the consequences or has not time to specify them. Volition is immediate and uncluttered; intention is unimpeded. There is no detailed explication or grounding of the situation. Because of the speaker's ruling and representative position, his commitment enters and disturbs political reality, even if its full meaning and consequences are yet to be revealed. Nevertheless, the covenanted and romantic prime mover is undoubtedly placing his hand once more on the wheel of history.

Only in wisdom after the event, may the asserted 'rightness' within a political persuasion at the time be affirmed. 'Rightness' as a claim before conflict or as an unconfirmed report from the field must give way before that which emerges 'from the flow of history and politics' subsequently. Assertion before *eventus*, the event contrived, follows not only from clarification or synthesis of general ideas or principles which press upon the decisionist but also from an examination of his values or precepts of conscience or conviction that he can do no other. For even if the 'inner determination' and firm beliefs are no longer intact and he decides not to pay the full price for his virtuous plunge into 'independent action' in pursuit of 'ultimate ends', he may well retain some stature as yet another responsible but failed leading politician with intentions: say, the designer of a comprehensive project for the reshaping of an *ancien régime* which for a time captures both ballots and the popular imagination.

VII

Blair can subject himself to objective realism and reality but, in continuing to define significant experiences, encounters and moments in terms of points of departure or new opportunities for new interpretations of his self and his political personality, new dreams and persuasions, he bears the unmistakable stigmata of the political romantic. For the romantic is essentially not in love with past ages and cultures but with what can through dream and imagination be captured and made anew. As renovator and innovator Blair is devoid of any sense of the past: he is no restorationist. Like Malebranche's God, he unceasingly seeks the salvation of mankind but only occasionally does he have the opportunity of intervening in their affairs. From a central position, with unchecked potency as lord of the ballots, analogous to that of the Deity, his inspired ego embarks systematic transformation of the political order as given. For the romantic as statesman imbued with universal longings is able if he senses or seizes his 'occasion' to make through what has been called his 'genial ego' a competing reality of his own to what prevails in the given intractable 'cindery' disorder. Through wish and imagination at the disposal of a protean sensibility, through exercise of a new-found political persona and decisionist vocation he finds that, aided by intelligencers and soothsayers, he can make up his own reality as he goes along. Moreover, he becomes aware that as illumined chosen subject he is bound by no seemingly committed engagement or position. The medium of politics is necessarily in flux. For we can make what we want, either, as Novalis insists, out of the accidents of life or, to cite Fichte, out of the Non-Ego. We can receive intimations of a world spirit and move on to higher planes of politics — for Blair the global or the Continental — achieve *tour de force* after *tour de force* within a global consensus. For the statesman life is lived as in *un roman*. Nevertheless it is not Blair the romantic, Blair the liberal, who makes the 'right decisions' but Blair the newfangled decisionist at home at last in the political world of friends and enemies. He is now inured to an arena in which a new liberal imperialism seeks conclusive settlements in remote regions. We may, however, be witnessing not an abandonment of but a new phase of romanticism.

For the romantic the world moves on and changes through fluctuations of states of mind, turns of fancy and imagination; shifting intimations and perspectives, endemic discussion and discursiveness unrelieved by dogma or decision, constant revisionary and transforming departures from what subsists — all stemming from the conversations and confabulations of a liberal society. It has indeed been maintained that it is only in an individualist, liberal community devoted to debate and criticism of the given social and political order that the dissident romantic can find, on the one hand, the space, the isolation, on the other, the discriminating patronage, the 'conversation', the affinities and the 'circles', in short, the conditions in which he may discover and prepare to exercise his plastic powers. Here are the occupants of the 'self-regarding' spheres, the 'disencumbered' or footloose selves, the lonely walkers lost in reverie, the 'genial egos' imbued with the world spirit for whom the state or community is a work of art to be envisioned or perhaps fashioned by the romantic subject if only he can seize the 'occasion' to project his own reality as an alternative order stemming not from a cause but from a creative unfolding of his own imagination.

Both romantic and liberal contend in a universe or pluriverse of values: both are discontented with 'the mess of centuries' and are unconstrained by what has been given. Each can be shallow in both critiques and action; each can be destructive of 'the creations of time'; each causes and provokes much resentment.

Characteristically, the liberal reforms while the romantic transforms or displaces. The liberal sets in motion currents of opinion or doctrine asserting individual or group self-direction, self-disclosure, self-enactment against established powers or privileges, closed orders, customs and routines which obstruct self-realization, free agency and choice. In order that truth is discovered by reason, the freest play of opinion and enquiry is to be permitted. Liberalism secures immunities from arbitrary and offensive authorities, sets up constitutional checks on them and seeks to accommodate political life in all its angularity and incoherence by devising man-made institutions, rules and procedures to effect the collaboration of autonomous, separate wills seeking public volition of common action.

Against liberalism's emphasis upon causation and rational reform in a progressive and improving world under beneficent natural and human law, sanctioning only such conflict as leads by discussion or dialectic to higher truths, the romantic instigator seeks to move politics to a higher plane. Politics is transformed not by close and sustained empirical inquiry, planning and specific arrangements and compromises, but through revelation of dominant values, imaginative intention, realization of fantasy, invocations of futurity. Agency or stimulus is the self-making, emotive response to the 'occasion' or opportunity revealed before it. Spiritual energy, flow of feeling are however ultimately subordinated to either political decision or rationalism. Romanticism is always subordinated to the real, to whatever political action ensues. Blair, the romantic, must always yield to Bush the would-be master of the field. Romanticism must always be ancillary; its interventions do not commit even its 'occasional' instigators.

Nevertheless, the romantic has his emergence not in another hour but in a contributory 'state of mind' on an 'occasion' on the day for personal, formative experience and achievement: the Righteous Invasion of Iraq to follow, say, The First Victory, the Second Victory, the Tranfusion of Nostrums, the Beacon to the World: Invocations of Futurity, and, not least, the Fulfilment of the Covenant with access to the hegemonic power of 'the great and powerful friend'. Blair's genial ego grasps the wheel of history once more, and hopes to change its course. A romantic feat, like that of the liberal breaking the cake of custom, may well become archetypally heroic. Or like Prometheus he may steal fire and be chained to a rock. Yet as a romantic he may move on to a higher plane than the politics, the reality which still subsumes him. In using the 'occasion' as a point of departure to another reality, he opens up the self to new modes of political action and being, the exploration of barely revealed potentialities, the enactment of dreams and fantasies, and, most important for the politician, the informing and fostering of a new range of intentions and projects. For Blair, intent on intending, Utopia is once more at hand.

VIII

To his departures and excursions or what he apparently calls 'his first order decisions' Blair brings an intensely moral perspective. The imperatives of an ideology have no hold on him. The crux comes in his increasingly agonized searches as a neophyte decisionist for an irrefutable *casus belli*: in his concurrent endorsements of a particularly ruthless intervention by Nato in Serbia/Kosovo without United Nations approval; for his shoulder-to-shoulder concert with the President's declared war on 'terrorism' from 2001; for the punitive action against the Taliban; finally among the changing justifications for joint military action against Iraq as an absolute enemy, the foe. All three of these concatenated and sometimes *post hoc* indictments, indeed incriminations, at the bar of liberal humanity are followed up by the launching of collective campaigns of redress and constraint essentially against the demonized political leadership of certain 'dangerous and ruthless men': Slobodan Milosevic, Osama Bin Laden and Saddam Hussein.

From this admixture of virtue and reflected military prowess Blair emerges as an inaugurator and prophet of a new variety of the 'just war': the 'first progressive war'. In his paper, 'The Doctrine of the International Community', delivered to the Economic Club in Chicago on 22 April 1999, the victor and spokesman of the Kosovo campaign by Nato announces the coming of the truly 'liberal war': specifically, armed and moral intervention by the 'International Community' against the dictators who 'visit horrific punishments on their own peoples in order to stay in power'. Appropriately enough the provenance of this idea of moral interventionism is American and means that only those governments should be recognized which have a 'legal' democratic constitution. In practice, writes G. L. Ulmen, what is 'meant concretely by "legal" and "democratic" is to be decided by the USA'. It is this doctrine of global intervention that is taken up post-World War I by both Woodrow Wilson and Secretary of State Stimson. Blair's liberal affinities with Bush have signal American roots.

In the order of things to come the 'International Community' in such gathered strength as it may in particular instances command, is envisaged as an active and positive righter of wrongs among not only states but also among other contending dominions and powers, on the presumption that the West has the power to impose its own values and standards everywhere. Thus, closure may be called on the old prudent principle of non-intervention when external interests are at stake or at odds. The world is set to 'rights' if necessary by active military virtue in the form of mediating, intervening or punitive expeditionary forces, prevenient or pre-emptive, seeking quietus or settlement of some kind: restoration, change of regime, tyrannicide, 'domestic' or 'external'. The end is no longer prudence but virtue or rectitude — 'the right thing' — through imposition of values, in particular, those contained, according to Blair, 'in the notion of community' upon the erring regime or 'failed state'.

Such is the augury. Within a global ethic 'humanitarian' wars may — after necessary amendment of the United Nations Charter — legitimately be waged. By effective military action or the threat of it despots may ultimately be coerced or deposed or even seen as deserving justifiable tyrannicide from outside. To John of Salisbury, Saddam Hussein would doubtless have appeared as analogous to the Devil's Vicar and, as such, necessarily to be slain. Virtue, as Henry Kissinger remarks, may be 'running amuk' but such pre-emptive, belligerent justice still remains possible rather than presumptive in the ultimate, 'liberal' wars of the twenty-first century.

Rhetorically and romantically the innovating *vox* is that of Blair, the inculcator, the righteous legislator in translation to an altogether higher level of international political conduct, messianic in range, fervour and sheer application. This is a Prime Minister with a vocation of at least Gladstonian persistence and persuasion. At the same time this adventurer of the spirit and the moral imagination, Blair, comes to terms with the exigencies of politics. Through his fortuitous concomitance with his 'neo-Conservative' American allies he makes his second acquaintance with the 'blood and iron' of reality. At work in him is neither dialectic nor the startling neo-imperialism of his powerful ally, apparently seeking, in theory and practice, the permanent disabling of obstructive 'rogue states', so designated, and the reconfiguration and democratization of much of the Middle East. Blair's conversion to pre-emptive strikes, exclusion and possibly tyrannicide seems at odds with his central preoccupation: the transmission and diffusion of the highest values.

Yet poised as he is upon the clouds of unknowing of an ethical foreign policy, Blair continues to concur in the harshest of means to ends that cannot for him to be other than ultimate consummations devoutly to be wished: the destruction of a nursery of global 'terrorism' in Afghanistan; the elimination of Iraq as part of 'the evil axis' and as 'rogue state' in possession, reputedly, of 'weapons of mass destruction' (so identified); the extinction of Saddam Hussein himself in all his iniquity, the recalcitrant force long identified by the Pentagon as the 'absolute enemy' and therefore ripe for pre-emptive strike. Each of these actions is to be fought not simply against a 'just enemy' but against a demonic adversary as replete with the *animus hostilis* as the partisan who gives and expects 'neither law nor grace'. These virtuous wars will be followed by the 'justice' of the victor. The antitheses and the antagonisms of the cultures or civilizations are so posited by Bush and Blair that we seem to be engaged in one of the culminating struggles of mankind. Despite all his moderating advocacy of multilateralism and liberal institutionalism in final settlements affording some measure of justice to a 'just enemy', Blair seems to invest his *vox*, trans-valuing energy and deepest 'sincerity' in the final battle itself.

Blair's sudden capacity for sustained enmity, his conviction that it can be 'the right thing', surprises in one with such a tendency to come to terms and agree, to fuse cries, causes and policies into the pudding-stone or rather *omnium gatherum*, a glossary, words for all occasions and audiences, for all ends immediate and ultimate. One does not expect such a devotee of either a conglomerate Europe or Anglo-Saxondom, such a 'world-besotted traveller', such a hopeful emissary of *détente*, oratorically to engender the 'violence of mind' entailed in protracted hostile enterprises. One can only assume that while partisan public utterance in open arena elicits both friendship and enmity, it gives particular consistency and duration to the latter. Or that behind the eirenic, unity-seeking front of this leader there lies the style of a recklessly venturesome ego liable to be engaged in headlong pursuit, not of grand theory, but of grand intentions.

In this positive emergence from indeterminacy Blair demonstrates the 'inner determination' and passion of Weber's monocratic 'independent leader' in a disordered pluriverse. The necessarily subjective actions stem from presuppositions, liberal and religious. There are, of course, romantic overtones to the ordained, covenanted stance and to the personal conviction of 'supernatural virtue' with all of which Weber's 'ideal type' will have no truck. Weber posits an initially unencumbered intention and an autonomy of politics involved in a ceaseless struggle for domination, perhaps for a 'tyranny' in an irrational *mêlée* of values. There is nothing hovering above the perennial conflict of righteous intentions. Yet the decisionist politician can choose his own ethical limitations, responsibly adjust his convictions to his apprehension of circumstances, play to 'the rules of the game'. But the ethic of responsibility, counsels of prudence, 'an opening mind' may well lose their countervailing force of persuasion in Weber's world of 'diabolical powers' or in a pluriverse in which Blair's engagement in Bush's campaigns of retribution and punitive re-ordering against absolute foes — to achieve ends which are ultimate — involves concurrence in policies of 'shock and awe'.

IX

Weber cares little for democratic ideas or institutions as such. They are useful only in so far as they produce as an end result qualitative, independent, political leadership, preferably with the personal gift of grace, capable through essentially liberal individualism — shades of Humboldt and Mill — of strong impulses and desires and principled historical deeds, taking up and defending fixed standpoints in the world of states. Thus the politician out of his own subjectivity gives meaning to the polity. As 'chief of men' he interprets his own experience, is realistic and down-to-earth, is possessed of an assessing eye for men, events and fortune. The populace sense his fitness to rule, take in the political presence or bearing, the character or the style, the *gravitas*, the *amicitia* or the cultivation of solitary eminence. The electorate are particularly concerned with his own self-understanding and the projection of his own cause. His following, solidified by effective decision-making and mastery over the party-state, endorses both conduct and intentions and trusts him to cast the die. They are aware that there is no substitute for success and that it may demand the dissolution of moral distinctions.

The 'inner voice and the inner constraint' of the ideal ruling monocrat are raised not only in the exigencies of domestic and foreign policy, not only in those open arenas, but also against adversarial or inimical tendencies at the heart of government itself. They grow like mushrooms in the dark or behind closed doors and in the end attain an upstart, encroaching unity within the bureaucracy. It does not stem from class, party or movement, from church or ideology; its origins are neither intra-state nor inter-state but lie within the apparatus of government. It is singled out by Weber as holding out a particular threat to the democratic state.

Weber acknowledges that in the modern state a neutral Civil Service is an indispensable and irreplaceable instrument for governing men. In Bismarck's Germany it has grown so potent that it is feared as a usurping political force in its own right. Its capacity as an instrument of rationality to accumulate knowledge, experience and technique, to calculate, forecast and plan, to impose methods and procedure is converting what has been a disinterested agency into an irresistible, autonomous domination with its own matured standpoints, goals and strategies. It is losing the habit of subordination, developing presumptions of its own and evolving its own 'statesman in disguise', its own not so hidden eminences. The only counter to or control over this unwelcome development towards disunity, according to Weber, is political. The bureaucracy, non-democratic in its very nature, must be mastered by legitimate, democratic, political authority standing for national life and action.

We can assume that Weber's hypothetical ruler reflects his own fear of the crescent power of the bureaucracy, in particular, of the higher policy-making executives of the state. As the maxim goes: 'He who has in hand the execution of measures is, in very truth, the master of them'. Those who actually carry out the project will cast off neutrality and reduce the political incumbents to honorific roles. As office-holders politicians may well revert to their former 'amateur' or 'notable' status and exist merely to authenticate in some esoteric or symbolic way the effective work of a sovereign public bureaucracy: indeed, the dictatorships that it must surely establish are more to be feared than those of the proletariat. Weber's dread of the coming of bureaucratic authority, however, goes wider than its displacement of political incumbents.

The great issue is how the seemingly inexorable advance of this indispensable agent and instrument of public administration, with its inevitable 'universe of little cogs, little men clinging to little jobs and striving towards bigger ones', with its all-embracing hierarchies, forms and structures, can be stayed 'in order to keep a portion of mankind free from this parcelling-out of the soul', from this supreme mastery which will, in practice, confer authority upon inept and timorous middle-class time-servers without the nerve or instinct for decision-making, unblest by that *charisma* that might give meaning to the regime and counter both depersonalization and routinization. It may well be that bureaucracy, speculatively, can strike up affinities with either monarchical or oligarchical orders and be progenitive of acceptable governance in political cultures yet to be, but it may turn out to be incompatible with exemplary leadership in a mass democracy. Only the potentially plebiscitary power of the Weberian 'ideal type', prime monocratic mover can save the political remnant within Parliamentary forms of democracy from encroachments of and possible displacement by a usurping bureaucracy intent on establishing autonomy and values outside popular control.

X

Incoming British Labour governments, it seems, always have misgivings about the Civil Service; over many years they posit an inbuilt class bias within the higher bureaucracy of the state against the representatives of the working class. Their 'middle- class abstraction' is seen to set them against the rising popular will which, if not aggressive or eruptive, may appear ill-informed or ill-advised as to policy or practice to the masters of process and procedure, possessed of all the facts. Skilled in assimilating up-country character or stubborn provincial virtue, concerned to avoid prolonged head-on collisions, still calling, I suppose, on their deep reserves of 'Ability in the Abstract', the mandarins must seem often to be erecting 'walls of experienced opinion' which the dusty victors of the electoral battlefield cannot immediately surmount. Nevertheless what appears unfortunately untutored in the style or stance of the new Minister and his juniors cannot remain inimical; it must be shaped and absorbed. It is the business of the higher civil servant to cultivate an acute awareness of the mind of the Minister and, in one way or another, transmit his conclusions to his colleagues.

Among other things, conservatism is a disposition and that there are certain predilections in the public bureaucracy towards a conservative temper or cast of mind cannot be denied. According to Karl Mannheim most impulsions come to servants of the state from outside and above and not from within where lie judgment and critique. The source of these instigations is Parliamentary: whether law or policy they enter the department through the Minister. His officials have their being and functions within an order bounded and prescribed by law, largely undisturbed by the immediacies of Parliamentary debate and collective partisan energies. The political 'intruder', to use C.H. Sisson's word, is not welcomed, and measures and policies are executed and assimilated into ongoing departmental conduct of administration without misrepresentation or modification to any significant extent of the prepossessions or intentions of the governing party. Even the Minister who before he has settled to his executive task may seem an 'intruder' and capable of divine intervention is, like God, soon reduced to the status of remote observer of processes long set in motion and long undisturbed. Within its accepted boundaries, writes Mannheim, '[E]very bureaucracy ... tends to generalize its own experience and to overlook the fact that the realm of administration and of smoothly functioning order represents only a part of the total political reality'. This closure of mind, this acceptance of the specific order in which all problems admit of an administrative solution, results in the prevalence of conservatism of mind and a disposition to take the world as it is or as it is constructively coming to be 'for granted'.

Bureaucratic 'conservatism' is no malformation. At varying depths it is occupationally and necessarily embedded in the enduring sediment of the administrative experience of the higher state bureaucracy; it is indeed fused into the professional wisdom, prudence, and proven critiques cumulatively gleaned in the diligent pursuit of a vocation as valuable to the polity as that of the impassioned, inner-determined and inner-constrained responsible politician. Indeed, it may be said the values of the matured and inured bureaucrat are more knowledgeably illuminated from within, more firmly grounded, than those of the politician casting around for moral imperatives, effective nostrums, reach-me-down cries and slogans in this value-laden world. Characteristically, the politician is a persistent intention, a venturing ego, seeking, in the public arena, echoes, applause and a following. His pumped up utterances result in sustained styles of animosity. And the end, as Hobbes notes, 'is not truth (except by chance) but victory'. The purpose of the public servant is not subjective but the defence of the general interest of the state by applying critiques to all political projects, enterprises and 'transformations'. Withal, his prime obligation remains that

of meeting the executive or administrative needs of any legitimate governmental requirement, programme or policy within
the compass of his department.

Blair does not specifically include the higher bureaucracy of
state among the motley 'forces of Conservatism' indicted in his
party conference speech at Bournemouth in 1999. Earlier, he
may promise 'a revolution in the machinery of government' but
that does not immediately diminish his utter dependence on the
administrative services of Whitehall for the realization of his
unrelenting, innovatory programme. Even a messiah needs his
bureaux. Here is the Rolls-Royce machine of the Civil Service,
the notable going concern, the eminently biddable formation,
hierarchical, experienced and creative, habituated to changing
political masters and political policies, to providing 'know-how'
and guidance at all levels and in all exigencies, to translating
prevailing values and imperatives into functions, structures,
indeed institutions – and rules.

Here is a bureaucracy just waiting for political domination,
any domination, traditional, rational-legal or charismatic. It
serves Churchill, Wilson, Heath and Thatcher, all sorts of 'inner
determinations', manifestations of the will-to-power – without
demur. Blair is sensed as a Prime Minister, at least as much if not
more determined than his predecessors. His intentions as a
transvaluer and refashioner of the *ancien régime* in Britain are
well known and arouse curiosity or excitement. Moreover, Blair
knows as well as the bureaucracy that even behind Britain's as
yet unreformed institutions, untrammelled power is still lying
unleashed. And do not intimates and followers already note in
the young aspirant to rule and authority a touch of Caesarism or
Napoleonism? Romanticism, however it seems is not diagnosed.
What is most noticeable about Blair's pattern of government is
its personalism and occasionalism. Persona dominates his
recourse, first to closet rather than open cabinet decisionism,
second to dramatic u*rbi et orbi* declamatory use of platform and
media to expound, illumine and attribute his instigation and initiatives, his able development of a 'presidentialism', already
intimated by his immediate predecessors. He hardly needs an
officious 'revolution in government'. Here is centralist, top-

down power seeking ends not only systemically innovatory at home and abroad but also 'ultimate' and even utopian. He needs neither 'this great party of ours' nor a 'charismatic' community. The grace, the values and the imperatives, the prowess are rooted in himself.

Habituated to impulsions and control from above, the going concern is available at any level Blair chooses to use it from the highest policy-making to the lowest forms of micro-management. Far from being cumbersome, inexpedient or impolitic, the Civil Service has long developed its own 'inner statecraft', prudence, discretion, flexibilities and aptnesses. True, its harboured continuities may not flow very freely into Blair's 'futurity'. It may not be at all keen on his activated values, especially his 'ultimate ends' and messianic vocation; in short, objections may be taken to the cut of his jib. But here is what Hegel would recognize as the countervailing and critical agency for pitting state 'universality' against the particularities, the subjectivities and interests of civil society. But while the bureaucracy not only administers but also defends the state against inimical ideas and forces — it exists to integrate what is given — it is also an enabling power which acknowledges the legitimacy of a new political intention and design, a fresh orientation on the world. Its own intentions remain 'universal' but it is not averse to 'a turn of the political imagination'.

It is therefore surprising that Blair — despite the facility of his rise to office and eminence, the conclusiveness of his installation as prime mover, his calculated accommodation of countering forces — experiences so much difficulty in setting the state and lesser bureaucracies in motion to realize his absolute but simple project. Despite the 'spin', the spells, the 'occasions', the compulsions to fulfil the long withheld or thwarted promise of Liberal-Labour fusion in an irremovable national party of government to undertake, not only the rebirth of the island kingdom but even the radical reform of the public services, seems to belong to the politics of dream.

Nor is Brown, the *de facto* Second Consul, with his Treasury tentacles spreading 'into every nook and cranny of social policy', with coercive controls through 'public service agreements' with all government departments, despite his vaunted achievements with the national economy and finances, faring so much better. Neither as grand policy-makers or as 'statesmen in disguise', nor as serried micro-managers has the Civil Service consistently pleased its political masters. A more insistent and sustained distinction between values and targets as energizers is frequently urged from above but, in New Labour practice, the first usually leads to the second. What is clear is that in the 'core-crunch issues' of the public services Blair, the manifold, discursive statesman, finds fewer occasions for realization of his 'genial ego' than *fortuna* makes available to his startling liberal *virtu* in international affairs.

Successful or not, this concentration, post-Kosovo, by the prime mover as agent of National Efficiency, Information and Enlightenment upon the reorganization and micro-management of the public services, necessitates the sluicing of huge sums of money, 'eye-catching' and eye-deceiving, from the Treasury, through the whole system of government. Rehabilitation of neglected public services not only means an uninhibited return to 'tax and spend' policies of a Labour 'elective dictatorship' on a scale to gratify the subdued cohorts of Old Labour who sense a reversion to an older socialist orientation; it also means a shot in the arm for bureaucracy in all its public forms for which the rehabilitation of the neglected public services cannot but bring in its wake intimations of better things to come in the way of numbers, salaries and esteem. *The Sunday Telegraph* points out, that, in Europe, Britain, 'the greatest engine of growth, carries the largest bureaucracy'. As 'enlightened despot', 'master of powers' and 'parts', withal romantic, the Prime Minister is staking the survival of his second government not on the subordination of the bureaucracy as a possibly inimical ascending force to the life — and fate — enhancing political leadership but on the creation of a 'Moloch to whom the life blood, not only of the present generation but that of posterity must be sacrificed'.

XI

'Without a powerful commitment to goals and values', maintains Blair, 'government is rudderless and ineffective however large their majority.' Just as surprising as his doubts about the ability of the *force majeure* of his Parliamentary following to achieve his mandate without complete engagement are his fears that a bureaucracy, so neutral, so prescient, so prevenient, so providential as the British may nevertheless perversely fail to accept the domination of a political intruder, so singularly possessed of 'supernatural virtue' as Blair. For he must be aware that there is nothing amateur, avocational or transient about this nineteenth-century corporate function, duty-bound to provide counsel, intelligence, watch and ward and all manner of undertaking services for the executive. Clearly this is an institution which has come to stay and is, as Weber would say, inescapable. 'There is no example of a bureaucracy being destroyed except in the course of general cultural decline.'

But because political well-springs may be diverted, political intentions blurred, objectives adjusted by rules, precedents, prudence and prejudice during the passage of policies or laws through the apparatus, an unusually highly committed government like Blair's New Labour, innovatory to the point of revolution, insists that government departments be monitored, guided and advised so that officials in their implementations and their undertakings do not modify the primary intention or party line in order to conform with the *genius loci* or with some random or professional bias or animus. The well-springs are to be kept clearly flowing from their source in Downing Street by stationing riverine water-watchers, deeply party-faithful, 'sea-green incorruptibles' actively engaged in and eternally vigilant bearers of New Labour's mission throughout Whitehall. They are installed as political or special advisers to see that the bureaucracy does not covertly get the upper hand and, at least as important, to ensure that, through manipulation of preferment in the press offices of the departments, in the publicising of the serried executive and legislative activities of this intensely party government the Whig dogs always get the best of it. In sum, the victors at the General Election are not to be frustrated by the wilful or refractory apparatus of government, mystified by harboured 'wisdom', assimilated to established continuities by an institution more experienced and, necessarily, more objective than themselves.

Precautions therefore have to be taken against bureaucratic influence and suasion at the highest level, against cumulative subversions by those *in situ* or in the corridors. Even behind closed doors there must be constant vigilance so that fidelity to political intentions and strategies be preserved. In short, it seems that it is not only the placemen but the civil servants who are to be controlled and, if necessary, undermined. So an ethos, a disposition, is paradoxically dissolved by an extraneous zeal. One presumes that not all the manipulation of the stationed monitors and undertakers is positively on behalf of New Labour as conflated, for a promised generation, with the British state. Some is surreptitious, stealthy and deftly protective of departmental conduct and name as such and not necessarily peculiar to the defence or promotion of a new secular order. The bureaucratic officers may merely be taking cover opportunistically:

> I have done one braver thing
> Than all the worthies did,
> And yet a braver thence doth spring
> Which is, to keep it hid

The scale and sustained intentness of those intrusions into the heart of the Civil Service, this successful capture of the beach-heads of communication of the departments indicates that Blair still harbours the suspicions of old Labour concerning the higher bureaucracy. Victory on the electoral battlefields is not enough. The enemy still has his redoubts on the commanding heights of government. Hence the recourse to the systematic planting of partisans in the apparatus.

At this point Blair would seem in all his singularity to conform to Weber's ideal type. Weber sees the crescent public bureaucracy as a threat to creative, individual political domination in the democratic state. Primarily, he fears that it will develop autonomous allegiance to values of its own, to political aspirations peculiar to itself. Weber and Blair agree that the public service must be subordinated to the political; its essence is instrumental. For Weber this is a theoretical problem to be countered in the future by individualist, egoistic, political virtuosity best assured by plebiscitarian democratic elections. For Blair it is a practical problem. Throughout his seven years' period of office he is irritated and frustrated by its inefficiency as an agent of transformation, despite personal admonitions and exhortations from on high, or invidious comparisons from time to time with business and even with the army.

It is, of course, yet to be revealed just how deeply the ascendant Blair 'idea' interpenetrates the Ministerial fastness or moves the hierarchies, just how the new impulsions from within rather than from without the departments are received. Do guided officials and instructed Ministers always display the alacrity demanded of them in what are, after all, revolutionary times? For charisma, remote and ineffectual in Whitehall, remains at a safe distance. And so, peradventure, delivery is delayed; so is deliverance. What Blair really wants is a bureaucracy transformed into 'a charismatic community'. And only a transfusion or perhaps a transvaluation from the *patria* can effect this. And Blair confessedly knows nothing of the *patria*. Like Weber but unlike Hegel, Blair does not respect the bureaucracy as representing the universal interest of the state — and *patria* — dispassionately and objectively but as an instrument to be bent to his political will, which seeks to bring into being, through a durable political settlement, a new country. In Hegelian terms the government department under Blair's regime is not a place where the 'particular', the interest, the faction, the party-political is subjected to the scrutiny and criticism of the 'universal'.

In his *Diaries*, R.H.S. Crossman notes the intense dislike with which civil servants regard 'people' brought in from 'outside'. Even private offices and PPSs are looked upon with hostility. Officials, apparently, approve of sole responsibility for the department being vested in the Minister simply because, with it, outside influence is minimal. Whether it is a matter of presentation, as such, the eliciting of favourable public responses for news good or bad, the broaching, easing or instigation of innovations, whatever the 'voltage' of the message conveyed or the political import of the undertaking, the intruding partisan agents of New Labour are very likely to operate most significantly at those creative points where, according to C.H. Sisson, 'political intention and executive requirements meet ... adding not a little complexity to the civil servants' professional obedience'.

XII

Institutions, the concrete orders of the British constitution are bent to Blair's will and need. The House of Lords, as far as can be seen, seems destined to become very much an ancillary, technical revising chamber largely made up of prime-ministerial appointees, with not even vestigial ground to stand on as order or estate or élite. Bicameralism itself, its form and functions, remains a matter for somewhat idle and remote speculation; its future in providing effective institutional checks on the House of Commons and on the executive remains undetermined. Decisionist governments, wary of delay by discussion and amendment, inconvenient checks and balances, cannot be expected to look favourably upon second chambers. Blair has a general liberal provenance but he now runs a truly political and democratic government which on its infallible course will not be thwarted. There can be no limits on the injunctions which derive from the highest values. The House of Commons, controlled by a majority who hold most of the seats because of Blair's electoral virtuosity, not only provide a constant and ultimate guarantee of dominance for New Labour but also the base for an optional fully-fledged 'elective dictatorship' if and when the need arises. The Civil Service, as we have seen, is openly and busily being brought under detailed control. The judiciary is to be 'modernized' so that it does not obstruct the new dispensation. The Lord Chancellorship, judicially and administratively the heir of the ages, is to be abolished not merely because its admixture of powers is a standing affront to liberal constitutional dogma but also because it seems egregiously and offensively 'archaic' to 'modernizing' rulers for whom nothing acquires objective value through the passage of time.

Whatever importance Blair may give to the 'separation of powers' there can be no doubt of his intention to concentrate the control of two of them, the legislative and executive powers, within his own hands. The prime mover within the state, he wishes to enjoy the same dominance, mastery of powers in office that he acquired over New Labour in the making in opposition. A General Election, for him, has done its job when it installs in power a hyperactive monocrat charged with bringing about a new order of politics not by healing coalition — although recourse to that may be in the Project again in the course of things, either as necessity or as *pis aller* — but through the dictate of a leadership virtually commissioned by *demos*. For the theology of politics demands decision one way or the other and such is surely assured to one who is master of both Parliament and the Civil Service and at the same time embodies a new political prejudice in the making. Two great national prejudices have long contended in vain to establish themselves, each in turn, as dominant. It is now time for the entrenchment of a third — oddly disclaiming the status of *patria* — from the middle way, an engrossing or excluding centre which chooses to designate the displaced Conservatives as 'the other', the indubitable enemy.

In the end, then, Blair's New Labour does not seek to make politics less adversarial, but, by identifying the foe, make them more so. His intention, informed and projected by intra-party complot, Blair, the Legislator — and Executive — seeks, not like Attlee or Thatcher, a new settlement but a re-orientation of Britain as a 'country' and a polity. Even in Britain, notably without legend of necessary executive reaction, personal or impersonal, in times of peace, such as persists in France and, *absit omen*, Germany, there are still 'moments' or perhaps even 'occasions' when the political imagination seizes upon the possibility of rousing 'the strong state' that slumbers within British constitutional arrangements. In the instance of New Labour it seems that such a recourse to ungathered strength invokes neither *patria* nor 'independence' but either the overwhelming patronage of great and powerful friends or fateful and nescient renunciation of *patria* within a puissant and prosperous European state.

With dominant Legislator duly entrenched in office, Tory Opposition, dispirited by crushing electoral defeat, powerful anti-Minister nowhere in sight — a Churchill or Enoch Powell —

what happens in Blair's first Parliament ceases to matter very much. With behind him a faithful if fortuitous Mountain of brute votes who regard him as the deliverer from interminable Opposition, Blair need not regard dissent or criticism from below as more than nostalgic or tribal unrest. For whatever insurgents gather to test Blair's ascendancy, no one can doubt that the Prime Minister has got the Maxim gun and they have not. For the arch-accommodater of parties and factions, the reconciler of nostrums and slogans, the master of the pliable as well as the passionate mode, the eirenic man in the middle, the master-politician, has at his disposal, especially in his second Parliament, an adamantine stance to confound those rebels who, on the floor of the House, venture to withdraw support for legislation or policies of fundamental importance, particularly those in which the integrity or prestige of the Prime Minister is known to be fully engaged. If he does not get his way he threatens to 'put his own office on the line'. Like Samson Agonistes he endangers the whole edifice.

Thus he makes it clear that he is more than *prima donna assoluta*. He is indeed 'the keystone of the arch'. In the end he is concerned neither with party nor with Parliament but with executive command over men and measures. He springs as he must from a liberal society and as a politician begins with liberal aspirations and attitudes, devises in detail a cross-bench liberal prospectus but in office shows little love of liberal institutions or 'the concrete orders' and professions that sustain them. His dream is of personal sovereignty of a reformed strong state driving towards a *political* consummation as an energizing and reforming force within an integrated greater Europe. His is a geopolitical romanticism centring on a regenerate Britain removed to a higher plane. Whatever emerges from this political imagining, Blair contemplates a positive determining role as a *persona* at the apex of the order or system and all the ascriptions that go with it: virtue, prowess, political prescience, legislative creativity and the power to decide — in all, signalling emergence from liberalism into politics.

XIII

Blair enters Parliament from another realm, from high colloquy or summit, from the country retreats of high diplomacy. In the House of Commons he is like a Visitor conducting a visitation. He is at home neither in his party which he uses instrumentally to achieve and retain office nor in the legislature through which he conducts his transformation of the body politic much as Henry VIII carried through his Reformation. He is not bone of Members' bone nor flesh of their flesh. He is the Outsider to whom the temper and the tone of the lower House must remain to a degree a matter of surmise. Clearly, he is not at all like, say, Balfour or Baldwin a devotee of the House as such, acquainted with the Members, as of a club, their tempers, conduct and histories — except in so far as they are documented in Downing Street dossiers. He seldom puts in an unobliged appearance in the chamber, takes part in divisions or stays to listen to unfriendly or unknown debaters. At Parliamentary Questions, which are re-scheduled to meet Blair's convenience, he is inordinately well prepared for the performance in rebuttal, denial and rehearsed response. Customarily, he eludes the substance of questions rather than 'answers' them.

PMQs, in his hands, turn from a means of defending and justifying his administration to an offensive serial campaign against particularized enemies on the 'shadow' front bench, directed to winning the next election. They are also an opportunity for deflating questioners from Opposition backbenches by citing, confounding or discrediting 'facts' about contexts or motivations, culled from rapidly compiled dossiers on presentations or persons. PMQs also afford occasions for expressions of loyalty to or reassurance for the Prime Minister from the rank-and-file faithful. From behind him the Ministerialist Mountain sedulously voice both their and their constituents' warm endorsements of the regime and all its works. With remarkable regularity and sustained vehemence Blair also uses the interrogation as a platform for denouncing, face to face, the Shadow Ministers of the Opposition; to baying approval from his following on the Floor he subjects them, one and all, to a repetitious rodomontade on the Government's achievements and the Opposition's past record of omissions, derelictions and failures. Thus does the House of Commons confirm its time-honoured, if now somewhat overwrought duty, 'to cheer a Minister'.

Persona, the celebrity, the smiling public man at the apex, in all his intention to establish 'what Tony wants', the subject in power *par excellence* but at the same time the object, the receptor of much adulation, some idolatry, divers ascriptions of unusual political talent. This is a personalist, decisionist ruler 'spliced' into the British state at its apex. At the very centre of White-hall-Westminster, Blair and his court enjoy uncontested power. The House of Commons continues to go through the processes of legislation and financial control, holds government to account, educates through general debate on national affairs, redresses grievances and so forth. For most of the time the Com-mons affirms and acclaims; in such a mastered and therefore receptive assembly, the ground seldom moves. There is very little possibility — has not been for a long time — of the formation of an autonomous will. The will is already formed or being formed in the Downing Street court or its purlieus. Like the bureaucracy the legislature serves an untrammelled executive. There may be a growing autonomy in the Select Committees; there may be rebel-lions on the Floor, but it cannot be said that the dominant will of the party-state is ever in serious peril. Procedure has been mod-ernized during this regime but, as in the past, never so effectively as to strengthen the Commons as an agency of control or point of attack so as grievously to embarrass the administration in the enactment of its programme. The Commons — notably more markedly than the Lords in their present anomalous condition — are merely an antechamber to the bureaux.

It is very doubtful if the Blair regime fully senses the nation, historic or emergent, through Parliamentary assemblies. Indeed it seems to prefer to do this through extra-Parliamentary institu-tions, either through focus groups and polls, or, more persis-tently, through the media, now the unchallenged, incomparable arena for political discourse — the collusive, concurrent, concat-enating continually at odds with the discordant, dissenting, dis-ruptive, the hostile and the inimical. From these polemical well-springs irrigating channels flow down to hydroptic fields of inchoate opinion, that public opinion which Peel characterized as 'that great compound of folly, weakness and prejudice, wrong feeling, right feeling, obstinacy and newspaper paragraphs'. Clearly, Peel is not intending to mine or tap it. Blair, however, is bent on extraction, through focus groups and pollsters, of serried opinionations of his persona, possibilities and prospects in order to amass yet another *omnium gatherum* in which veins of coherence and consistency may be traced and converted into intelligence. The centralizing Caesarean ruler is informing himself and keeping in touch by recording divinations, snatches of common sense, prophetic utterance and conjectural history. Consulting the populace, its apperceptions and apprehensions, deriving political touchstones from 'the great debate' enables Blair to conduct in forum a plebiscitarian kind of politics studded by decisive General Elections, without spending much time in Parliament. Not only does he in this way gather a cluster of touchstones upon which his 'eye-catching initiatives' will be based; he also achieves an intimate, sentient, presence *vis-à-vis* 'the nation' as assembled in focus and communes with it subjectively and histrionically, so much more effectively than he may with the body politic in the Commons.

XIV

As presence, as persona, Blair brings to the premiership the shock of the novel, the unexpected. For he is not borne to office by some explicit movement in party or country, set against mere incumbency, calling for mastery of powers and the installation in office of the lonely reconstituting virtue of some rare political being. His is not the elevation of some purposive, shaping statesman, possibly Anti-Minister, to dispel protracted public anxieties, determine undetermined ends, solidify the flux. Blair's endowments, his 'gifts of fortune' are doubtless assessed. So too his potentialities, his prowess, manners and *vox*. What is foreseen of his promise is enough to assure what is recognized by the party as a felicitous accession to the leadership. Prime Minister Blair, then, despite his singularity, is not 'a sport of history'.

Neither, however, is he, what Bolingbroke calls 'a standing miracle'. This is what the British have never really wanted as their ruler. Sufficient unto the day is one with a consistent will to govern, a capacity to know the next thing to do and ability to make and enforce decisions, an unchallenged integrity, a talent for self-clarification, and self-identification with the nation's history. As renovator, innovator and transformer, as world and European statesman, Blair cuts a dash that moves him to a plane well above that required for exacting these minimal attributes. Yet his sense, in Bertrand de Jouvenel's words, of moving 'like a joyful striding giant', surely cannot endure. The 'restless innovator' must be cut down to 'dutiful incumbent'; the country will then be content to be at ease with itself; drift will replace mastery. Allegiance must shift. 'A voice moved men and now it has lost its virtue and another is listened to.' The proclaimed renewal of political energy and ambitions is subsumed into the repertory of governance and, in the end, becomes only a brief chapter in the narrative of the short historian.

For despite the long gallery of platform politicians in modern times, Britain has, in a peculiar way dispensed with the formative governmental impress of 'great men'. 'We have', writes Ernest Barker, 'many leaders but not, as a rule, a leader'. Perhaps the propensity to avoid political virtuosity or unusual sway set in long ago under the influence of Edmund Burke's tortuous ruminations on the calibre of British politicians. 'Great men' are not always reliable, not always available. In our own time both historians and political scientists have remarked how since World War I, and indeed since long before, the relative absence of *legenda* of formative domestic statesmanship in times of peace in Britain. Gabriel Almond notes that in the British political system, 'in many significant historical episodes, in its more dramatic manifestations', leadership simply does not appear. The developmental pattern of the British system notably involves 'incremental-adaptive forms of change'. He speculates on the possible existence in Britain 'of a kind of counter-leadership cultural mechanism'. *Pace*, Max Weber, in Britain there has been a paucity of unusual and innovative leaders to discover and create new options to mobilize and combine 'new and old resources in creative ways' — to make fundamental and durable choices. It is also remarked by John Vincent how, between the wars, no great party in Britain succeeds in placing in office 'a single directing intelligence' also capable of 'some very general act of the imagination ... a man obsessed with the present as a basis from which to create a future'. So the chance 'of marrying the power of the parties and the power of the state, of taking from the world of party politics a unifying intelligence ... and placing it astride the system of meaningful action' is lost.

Doubtless Blair would regard himself as the answer to just such a paucity. Yet he finds himself after seven years of office not only unappreciated for what he considers his achievements at home, undervalued, and even indicted for his military ventures abroad but also irked and agitated by the widespread decline of the regard and trust in which he is held at large. Under his regime the British Constitution seems to be losing not only its reputation but also its adaptability and usefulness. The 'concrete orders' of the Constitution, Lords, Commons, Civil Service, Judiciary and their underpinning professions and vocations are at odds with New Labour and its movement to untrammelled authority. Bicameralism, its form and functions, has become a matter for speculation on persisting institutional neglect. Its future as an institutional check on both Commons and Executive is uncertain. The sheer ineffectiveness of open 'rational suasion' on the Floor becomes increasingly disquietening to the public. Procedure, 'the only constitution the poor Englishman has', remains as mysterious as ever. The advent of New Labour with its conclusive, non-heuristic, prophetic programme sharpens Parliamentary enmities with the Tories, in particular, and weakens that implicit consensus among the parties (a Blairite desideratum) that alone may prevent the emergence of the congealed party-state with its inimical solidarities and imperatives. For this has become a decisionist regime intent upon minimizing the power of the House, Ministerialist or Oppositional, to delay by discussion, compromise or amendment the imperative business of the prime mover. Limits to government are built into liberal structures but none into injunctions which derive from values.

XV

The emergence under New Labour of a truly polarized, *political* and *democratic* government, claiming to fuse the interests of ruler and ruled and impressing at the outset a new identity upon an ancient polity is a remarkable culmination of a political movement steeped in ideas which are basically liberal. Amity, consensus and co-operation among the parties lie at the heart of the Blairite moral reorientation. The nation is weakened by vigorous verbal strife between contending coherences, exclusive allegiances to disparate vital forces. Politics should dispense with its sustained antagonisms and much of its drama. Mrs Thatcher stands for confrontation, angularity and the primitive in politics. The day for the mediating centre has once more arrived. From Blair indeed there may have been expected a form of government not very different from that adumbrated by the Alliance coalition of the 1980s: a coming together of Parliamentary leaders, half-prised out of their convictions and political shells, semi-detached from their ideas and interests, displaying uncommon good sense, content to fuse talents and programmes. Politicians of the Centre will temper their certitudes, remit their theories, if they have them, to the realm of the speculative. What is expected to emerge is a mutual adjustment of partisan energies through compensations, manipulations, reciprocities and the like under the 'central coordination' of 'pivotal' politicians.

Practice, particularly 'the best practice', dissolves obstructions; *'force majeure'* triumphs but insidiously, politely, gratuitously, with ideological competitors on left and right excluded from office and with the centre no longer obliged to engage in 'hypothetics', politics move on to a higher plane. Such are the dreams and stratagems of the middle kingdom. The Alliance does not live to enact or realise them. New Labour embraces *Realpolitik* and outgrows them; concedes, under Blair, that there is no political struggle without predicament that liberalism itself is a critique of rather than a theory of state and politics. Doubtless, there persists among liberals a hankering after some change in opinion that will give to the *politiques* of the middle in fusion or coalition such dominance as will ensure a liberal regime under a junta of 'wise and politic' oligarchs. Once more there will be 'twelve million Jenkinsites standing by'. This does not happen. It is significant that the Project devised by the New Labour cabal deep in Opposition to fashion a Centre Bloc with a fusion of Liberal Democrat and Labour parties in the event of a close result in the General Election of 1997 comes to very little. The liberal and Blairite dreams of a new mediating political dominance and the consequent consignment of the Tories, existential opponents of Liberalism, to the rump-status of oblivion comes to nothing — as does Proportional Representation as an electoral enterprise destructive of the historical dualism within the party system. It is as though in his military phase — five wars in six years — Blair's liberalism becomes recessive.

XVI

When the *Daily Telegraph* presents Blair as 'an able man with a serious purpose' the writer is presumably identifying a political talent undertaking the hotfoot transformation of a country of which he must have despaired. As radical, liberal and Labour, Blair pits a rampant rationalism against the reality that has come to be and sets out on a fame-seeking, revolutionary and destructive course towards plateau after plateau of self-consciously elevated 'modernity'. As a romantic he also seeks 'occasions' to project wish and dream; as such, like the liberal, he contends with the reality of the extant order. The enterprise as a whole is liberal. It starts with individual self-disclosure and self-enactment in the world, performance rooted in belief. It ranges itself against dogma and establishment, it breaks the cake of custom. This rejection of what is requires the agency of heroic, perhaps Promethean, leaders.

As a war-lord, Blair may well have been comparatively untouched by American 'Neo-Conservative' Caesarism, military realism in the Middle-East, but he certainly seems to have moved away from persistent liberal dialectic that seeks to eliminate the truly political: the capacity to decide who is the enemy within and without. Liberalism has difficulty in conclusively determining and mobilizing. It is unsafe because it recognizes the legitimacy of a plurality of intentions and designs and is not good at closure. With inimical solidarities, conflicting political virtues, 'clear and present dangers' it often cannot cope. Whereas the core liberal institution is the debating chamber as an arena of equally valid ethical claims, stumbling discursively and incrementally towards a characteristically acceptable but undetermined future and amicably digesting dissent and divergence on the way, modern democracy is no longer at ease with mere discussion and technicalities, the slow grinding accommodations of Parliament; it has little faith in Benthamite sparking and conflict of ideas as productive of policy and action. The enemy should be defined and defeated. Politics should be consequential. Unlike liberalism, democracy is not intrinsically at odds with autocracy whether in the form of 'commissioned' or 'elective' dictatorship. For, ideally, it seeks not an unfolding world but, vainly, one resolved.

Such is politics seen from the Weimar Republic between the wars — with longing for Wilhelmine certainties. Something like these views may have dawned upon the still unformed Blair when 'going to the wars'. He becomes aware that enmity is not ephemeral; it is, indeed, the touchstone of political experience. The essential conflict is that of crescent solidarities seeking dominance. Caesarism is perhaps not for Blair but it is not impossible that in the event of a third victory at the polls he will incline, as a decisionist, to contemplate and define enemies as well as friends, domestically as well as abroad, forsake consensus and the Third Way, abandon his romanticism for the time being, become a resolute Executive and relay the truly political foundations of the state — an appropriate conclusion for a Weberian struggle for power with plebiscitarian democracy within sight.

Thus may Blair emerge not so much as an 'elective dictator' but as a 'commissioned dictator', 'a single directing intelligence' astride the system. He is the truly inclusive prime mover, the master-builder of eclectic politics at home, selecting at large from what he chooses to regard as the best practice in British politics in recent times: from Fabianism, Wilsonism, Thatcherism, Social and Liberal Democracy, with a dash of Christian Socialism, Hans Kung and Tom Paine thrown in. After the Third Way, no one should be surprised by further pillage of past tenets and persuasions. So despite a marked distaste for the accumulations of the past Blair becomes the heir of the decades, if not of time. New Labour that succeeds Old Labour now assumes the label of Syncretic Labour in which all the discordances of time-worn tenets, suasions and cries are reconciled.

But, as intimated, the Blair of the wars and high diplomacy is possibly a changed being. His mission is now essentially political rather than discursive or rhetorical. Blair is now among the dominions and powers. He emerges as proponent of active military virtues, the prophet and initiator of liberal 'just wars'. He enters into the realm of *hubris*: he takes risks and invites disaster. He is familiar with the *ultima ratio regum* and moves with ease between the hegemonies. In harbouring so much *enmity*, in engendering so much *resolution* in his pursuit of virtue and imposition of values on distant countries he becomes a leader well within the ken of old Europe.

To the liberal mind that flourishes at least as vociferously among members of the Labour party as among Liberal Democrats there is something most unpleasant about this strong conception of politics in which polarities are ultimately rooted in entrenched friendship and enmity. Can it be that Blair, the initially liberal political actor, finds himself obliged, in order to achieve efficacy and authenticity in a world of contending values, to go below the deep civilizing sedimentations of liberal society? Can there really be a primordial experience capable of emerging to govern subsequent experience and conduct? Is politics still concerned with reaching the commanding heights from which 'the other' may be dominated or negated?

XVII

It is important that a central, informing and activating bias of Blair, which governs both his 'enlightenment' and his political drives be noted. Blair has no 'idea' of the separateness of England from Europe. He does not recognize the inherent autonomy of England as a power and a culture, is not aware of the fact that, according to Friedrich Heer, she has considered herself since the eighth century — more than Gaitskell's 'thousand years' — a different world from Europe: 'an *alter orbis* circling the Continent like the comet in the Bayeux Tapestry'. The insular spirit as reflected in her political institutions, theology, political thought and economic theory constantly diverged from that of Europe. Europe was a place where Englishmen periodically 'went to the wars' and 'tried their luck' or sustained a balance of power. As a maritime power with universal dominion, singular England distinguished itself from the land-powers of Europe navally, commercially and imperially. Englishmen, in particular, have long defined themselves by differentiating themselves from Europeans, and, in order to retain their independence, have done their best to confound, divide and balance them.

British statesmen, apart from Blair, seem recently to have some difficulty in finding and drawing upon a 'usable past'. Ian Robinson and David Sims note in the unknowing 'revolutionary', Edward Heath, that there is a singular 'disconnection from the British past' especially from the tradition of continuity and change within the British Constitution, 'a blankness' about Conservative 'policy'— an inauthenticity that cannot but end in panic, appeasement and eclipse. Like Blair, he is condemned to act in what he hopes is a manageable present, to look forward to a futurity in which an independent Britain is absorbed into a European polity, commitment and identity —resistance to which has helped to form the British *patria* over centuries.

Conservative and New Labour, Heath and Blair, are both Outsiders: neither responds to any gravitational pull within the country; each wishes to subordinate Britain to a wider prudence. Each contemplates fusion into the European polity as an achievable *fait accompli* locking a British province into a community speculatively constructed in Messina and Rome by alien will and artifice. Even as the Outsider, Blair is aware that Britain is not a *terra nullius* to be absorbed into a richer, more potent union. A European by conviction, he considers — like Macmillan, Heath and George Brown — that Britain brings to Europe not just long experience in a stable, successful political 'tradition of confidence' but also proven diplomatic skills and even gifts of what Europe, as the prototypical continent of states, has surely never been short: statesmanship. What Blair, firmly ensconced at the 'heart of Europe', her potential President, a political talent operating on the highest plane, offers from eminence and celebrity is international statecraft.

Statesmanship has always had its difficulties in a country where the collegiate governing mind — mediating, moderating and heuristic — has always tended to be 'brooding and concocting' rather than to be given to the generation of large designs and strategies. But Blair obviously breaks the mould. And who has a better base, a safer seat at the high table of proliferating Europe with 'new' members asserting themselves against 'the old gang', a better ascendancy over his electorate through his large single-party majority and his consequently indefeasible means of getting things done domestically without harassment, than the British Prime Minister? For in him, according to state of mind, is the illumined capacity to seize the secular moment, the opportunity or 'occasion' for 'making a future out of the present'. Who better 'to navigate on the stream of time', better to provide leadership in drawing up the *nomos* of the globe than Tony Blair, the hero of Kosovo and Chicago and of Congress?

Here then is the Single Separate Power, the Intruder or Outsider, a political force imposed by the unrelenting democratic process — 'a dynamic force' said Baldwin, 'is a very terrible thing; it may crush you, but it is not necessarily right'. Here is a British statesman not at all content to steer with modest intentions. His is not one of those surprisingly creative leases of office, one of those regimes that will creep into fruition through accumulation of meditated measures, resumption of forgotten initiatives, by virtue of latent ministerial talents and their consonance with bureaucratic abilities, and in which threads of consistency and persistence are more discernible than design. What Blair exhibits is personal prowess within a distinctive 'system of conduct' that enables him to display or 'spin' a kind of mastery and effect a closure of favourable opinion behind him. Although the project seems to have been partly liberal in provenance, the style becomes monocratic. As such, it manifests illiberal tendencies and in the course of effective action tends to protect itself from destructive criticism and disabling discussion. 'Spin' insists that

New Labour is not fallible. After all, the governing will, the capacity to make and enforce decisions, stems from two General Elections which have been plebiscitarian enough to meet Weberian desiderata.

The political conduct of Blair then meets not a few of Weber's requirements, indeed prescriptions, for effective individual political leadership in a modern democratic state. The political struggle, which determines who dominates, takes place on the same Weberian stage of contending universal values in an irrational pluriverse. It is only as the slave of the victorious passion that a settled rational order emerges or prevails through the active, independent politician chosen and trusted by *demos* as he who makes a successful stand for a prejudice and legislates for the enactment or execution of the imperatives emerging so lucidly from it.

Blair too is recognisable in the Weberian conviction politician, possessed of core values if not core doctrines, the passionate advocate of new orders and emergent causes. His is an unmoored subjectivity which finds office and eminence and fields of action. He is the antithesis of the mollusc finally settled upon his rock. Mere incumbency is not for him. For as one of the qualitative few who see into their own time Blair, like Alexander Hamilton, another fame-seeker, seeks 'a degree of power commensurate with the end', a long lease of the ruling prerogatives necessary for extensive and arduous enterprises in the world. Weber thinks that politics gives 'meaning' and purpose to the world through goal-setting, decisionist leaders seeking the resolution of conflicting values when neither objective judgment nor effective mediation is possible. There is no moral framework; there is no sustaining history or legend. He is dismissive of liberal values, but despite all these negations and indifference to a fragmented Christianity, he believes in moral autonomy and responsibility. He is deeply concerned with the fate of the German state. The inner-determined individual, perhaps daemon-possessed, in observing the constraints of prudence, circumstances and morality in general conjured by Weber continues to operate within a rigorous secular frame of responsibilities. It is perhaps not easy to see how the protean Blair, self-revealing, sentient, heart-upon-sleeve, religious romantic, liberal right-thinking, discursive and 'occasionalist' fits into this Procrustean bed.

XVIII

There are many elements in Weber's 'ideal type' that, bereft of any conceivable influence or tutelage, find other than echo or resonance in Blair's conduct, indeed in his sustained performance as the mainspring of British government. Nevertheless, there is one presumptive central activity of statesmanship, one presumptive virtue with which he is not endowed. The one preoccupation of traditional statecraft which finds no persistent *vox* in Blair, which, presents no moment or 'occasion' for his talent, one locus which he does not seek to occupy, one allegiance to which he does not give primacy and that is the *patria*. Blair, the singular ruler seems to have no impalpable *patria* — except possibly for the *regnum coelorum* — seeks community but has no idea of the British 'community of character'. His focus lies not in the island as such but in the great globe itself.

Although Weber starts off in the Wilhelmine National Liberal tradition he breaks with it and becomes an uncompromising nationalist as such, if not *tout court* — he remains attached to a liberal society and liberal culture if not to 'liberal values'. His nationalism is presumptive and assertive; he believes in the territorial state with an assured monopoly of the means of violence; as a conservative Bismarckian what he hopes for most is a proficient general staff. It is even more important for a national leader to dominate a unified nation than a Parliament. The national state is delimited neither by ethical nor liberal values. Nor does it require an ideology, a mystique or a halo. 'I am', says Weber, 'religiously absolutely unmusical'. A religious person, like everyone else, must submit to fate. From the outset Weber is, as Richard Bellamy notes, at ease in a pluriverse of *Realpolitik*. Politics is a craft to meet the existential needs of *Reichstaat* and *Volkstaat*.

Nationalism, while it may be overwhelmed with doctrine and assume modes of action beyond the contemplation of the patriot — it tends to have an unfolding will and engage in missions in the world — is at root the *patria* rooted in a particular community, not within tribe, *polis*, principality, monarch or empire but within the *natio*. Weber's 'ideal type' leading politician cannot but stand for frontiers, for power, culture and *patria* in all its palpable and impalpable varieties, for the psychic roots of Germany. Weber's ideal cannot be other than a patriot statesman contending for coherence in a value-ridden and therefore irrational moral world. (Blair is the 'Napoleonic' internationalist similarly engaged.) For Weber is a polemicist as well as an academic, an occupant of the platform as well as the chair. The value-free sociologist acknowledges certain subjective values as unassailable, indeed existential, and invulnerable to objective critiques. As, in practice, a Conservative paternalist, he is passionate about the ideas which possess him, the goals set for the German state. Yet these values and ends are not absolute. They are limited by the ethic of responsibility and the realism of the leader. What matters, however, is neither moralizing nor 'liberal values', but the will to power.

It is surprising that it is on the high claim of the *patria* that Blair notably falls short of the ideal. For if any idea is particularly attractive to a fame-seeking subjectivity choosing focus, mooring or 'occasion' providing access to eminence and renown, it is surely patriotism. As Meinecke insists: 'The human being needs the community to sustain him and receive his contributions in turn … of all the great spheres of life that a man can enter, there is probably none that speaks so directly to the whole man as the nation'. The non-ego in all its posited variety and vastness is surely just waiting for formative interaction with the subject as ego, as creative formative imagination.

For a politician of liberal and eirenic provenance like Blair, seemingly a committed internationalist with no great devotion to the nation-state as such, patriotism, as what Sidgwick calls 'the less comprehensive affection', must seem the more acceptable sentiment, the more sober moral commitment than nationalism. For most of the time it remains unspoken, as part of the 'givenness'. For this there is no covenant; indeed, commonly, it does not go beyond customary approbation. It need be no more than an unforced endowment of a political persona; is less strenuously egoistic than nationalism. The patriot-politician is not obliged to belong to the 'spiritual priesthood' of the country; he need not emulate Stanley Baldwin.

Blair shows little interest in either cherishing or defending the British givenness. As a liberal he cannot accept it without stipulations. Whereas for Weber, and presumably for his exemplary political leader, devotion to the German Reich in all its manifold puissance is a first principle and duty, Blair, in pursuit of fame and regardless of the fate of the *patria* to which Weber's statesman devotes himself, uproots himself from merely insular obligations and engages in international liberal enterprises; in salvationary military interventions beyond the seas, against those sensed as *foes* or absolute enemies. The role of active patriot, interpreter and articulator of the British nation's experience in time, defender of the insular area of necessity, is replaced by the proponent and exponent of the universal, perhaps never-ending, 'humanitarian' or 'liberal' just war. From now on, we may assume, Blair 'responsibly' keeps watch and ward over perhaps 'impossibilist' ultimate ends in pursuit of vision and virtue.

Unmoved and unpledged by *'tout qui dure'*, Blair does not conceive of himself as the *gardien* of any rooted and obdurate *patria*. For Blair, Britain is not the indispensable prejudice but the wayward essence to be pooled in the Continental reservoir or the refractory fragment to be clamped into the European agglomeration. Blair has ultimate affinities, attachments and subordinations but they seem to be undetermined — matters for speculation. First, from his eclectic, perhaps heterodox, religious connections we may posit a subjection to the *regnum coelorum* as an ultimate *patria* from which we can assume both Christian reflection and the self-conscious pursuit of moral ideals. His former Downing Street Director of Communications insisted that 'we don't do God here' but Blair certainly does. Secondly, he sees himself as a maker, sustainer and servant of a new secular world order peopled by a responsible International Community, active, cooperative and frontierless, bent on achieving and enforcing a primarily liberal and humanitarian consensus. Each of these attachments is remote, impalpable and aspirational, poised high above national *patriae* and sub-*patriae*, palpable and impalpable, within that potential superstate of Europe which Blair acknowledges as his third attachment.

For as 'a believing European' he undoubtedly conceives of Britain as a leading component of and active agent in the construction of Europe as a new power among powers in the world. As far as can be seen this is a secular enterprise. Blair is not of a mind to underpin the foundations of this emergent bloc or hegemony with a sedimentary stratum of Christendom. Indeed the prehensile and now deeply *political* Blair, ever fertile with ideas of union, may well, with changing prospects, prefer to project the EU, furnished with its newfangled constitution, as a culmination of Social Democracy, a union of social democracies in which, deprived of its insular, dysfunctional, 'racist' nationalism, Britain may well contend for some kind of presidential leadership. Such an event might seal Britain's allegiance to a European *patria*.

Yet another distant affinity, liberal and impalpable, may arise from the image of the open-necked, triumphant war-lord of Kosovo celebrating his Nato campaign as an initial chapter in the making of a new potency which culminates in a venturesome engagement to extirpate terrorists from the face of the earth. This is a dedication which propels Blair into the wars as the destroyer of 'axes of evil', advocate of regime change, the imposer of liberal values and institutions on recalcitrant civilizations. This is the Blair who emerges from the conflict as a kind of liberal imperialist — shades of Asquith, Grey and Haldane — collaborating with American Neo-Conservatives, so named, in nation-building in Afghanistan and Iraq.

The attribution or ascription of this imperial role to the sentient, moralizing Blair essentially liberal *tout court*, seeking out suffering situations, emotionally 'scarred' by much of the televised human condition — in colour — is hardly apposite or appropriate. For he is no imperialist and has no obvious link to the British Empire as *patria*. A politician of his sensibility at the end of the nineteenth century is more likely to have taken up with the Little Englanders than with, say, Rosebery's Liberal Imperialists. And, in truth, Little England is never any kind of *patria* — are not Little Englanders notoriously 'friends of every country but their own'? Are they not, characteristically, moralizing 'public persons', acting like Blair *and* Cook, within an ethical framework and reaching confidently down to certain sentient, psychic roots of the liberal nation to arraign or criticise British imperial activities and values. Protean Blair can play any part. On other occasions he is not obliged to cleave to 'greatness', to side with hegemony and dominance. Personally, he is at least as well equipped to play the part of Anti-patriot as John Morley, Leonard Courtney, J.M. Robertson or J.A. Hobson, the late Victorian Little Englanders, all of whom doubted the compatibility of 'patriotism' with the liberal mind.

What matters to Blair is not so much the cause, the commitment, the pursuit — 'As I went down the waterside. None but my foe to be my guide', not even the operative decision — these must remain in the keeping of Bush. To Blair belongs the venture, the new departure, the imaginative self-definition, the self-enactment. But it seems that he needs the larger sphere, the larger community to receive his loyalty and his stimuli. For he is one of those autonomous personalities who, the more singular, innovating and indeed, autarchic they become, 'the larger the spheres', writes Meinecke, 'of their receptivity and influence can be'. It is clear indeed that he has not only outsoared his British political milieu and, as destructive liberal, mangled its liberal institutions; he is also content to consign Britain to the status of *sub-patria*, with nothing impalpable to defend, provincialised and even regionalized within a superstate.

XIX

Blair is not out of a mould. There is no political lineage and no sustaining political tradition claims him. He springs neither from established nor dissenting church, neither from Damascus road nor secular revelation, but from the accidents of life and education within a liberal society such as youthful play-acting, sixth-form critiques of the *mores* or institutions in which he finds himself, impatience for the transformation of immediate circumstances, fertility in suggestion for change; from imaginative, perhaps fictive, excursions into wider modes of experience, romantic departures from reality, self-confessedly from 'the age of colour television'; from undergraduate ventures into extra- curricular often religious discussion, earnest participation and fellowship in transient 'circles', populist performances on the guitar. One senses that he is always lighting on or departing from one discursive experience after another, one state of mind after another.

An independent individual, he is separate from and both instinctively and rationally critical of the order about him — already there are intimations of the constructive and destructive political rationalism to come with its animus against what has been made by the dead hand of the past. The demolition of the British Constitution is already looming. Behind this 'destructive element' there seems to be no distinctive, shaping, 'mind-blowing' cultural influences; he is relatively unburdened with nostrums. One remarks only a sustained irritancy, spleenish furiosity, running to rodomontade, with 'the mess of centuries' and the Conservative party.

Blair's intellectual hinterland is not impressive. Roy Jenkins is to pronounce that he has 'a second-class mind'. Yet from the beginning he attracts attention. Dominant is the desire to please and, in all encounters, to keep up an affable front. Clearly he does not own the device *Je maintiendrai*; he has no great inclination to defend anything; he is on no watch and is lightly encumbered with loyalties. Yet he is early aware that he has a bent for initiation, instigation and persuasion, and ultimately perhaps for 'leadership'. How and where he does not know; nevertheless, it must have swiftly borne upon him throughout his youth that his is a talent to be used. As a leader he pragmatically poises himself for unspecific success, perhaps eminence. As a liberal he expects to be caught up in the rhythm of an uninterrupted movement subsuming his talent both for self-direction and for co-operation and compromise with divergent wills.

Although Blair by design rather than through fate starts as the liberal rationalist renovator of an *ancien régime* installed in office by *demos* under the device of New Labour, his commission does not delimit him. He remains a trafficker in eventualities and individual destiny, a romantic occasionalist. As prophet, theorist and practitioner of the liberal 'just wars' of the twenty-first century, he necessarily assumes the persona and vocational role of the decisionist monocrat — he who, *ex nihilo,* terminates the discussion and plunges into the deed. The essence of politics from now onwards is not reconciliation but enmity. His liberalism seems recessive. Nevertheless he is still reproached for indeterminacy. This is because he has not been able, as liberal or romantic or as realist decisionist, to impose a single meaning on himself. As a persona he is unresolved: as a pluralist liberal with monistic tendencies he loses coherence. From now onwards he becomes an Outsider, outside liberal democracy and still outside the British canon or tradition simply because he has not done what T.S. Eliot calls 'the great labour' necessary for inclusion. It is still not possible 'to set him, for contrast or comparison among the dead', either aesthetically or politically, *sans* political genealogy, unencumbered by the past, perhaps not at home in the milieu he is making. Blair has not yet sorted out what John Gray would call his 'matrix of possibilities'. The leader who 'plays the part' fails to achieve a durable meaning either of character or style. It is, after all, writes Gray, 'not a question of what sort of life my nature demands but which of the many natures latent in my nature do I adopt as my own'.

Indicative of Blair's irresolution before casting his die is his tendency to entertain and play with political concepts or operative ideas and use them as abstract counters in the mysterious resolved dialogue or diallage of the Third Way in which discrete, political cries or nostrums, sometimes conceptual antinomies, acting in yoke, tandem or fusion, synthetically, symbolically or transcendentally, in or out of context, are brought into consonance or concert with each other without apparently blurring expression or cogency or mangling meaning. Quite obviously, this path through the middle offers a tool or technique for the discretion of a modernist pragmatic 'decisionist' at the centre moving neither left nor right but forward on to the high plateaux of futurity. The tone and temper are generous, liberal-left seeking reconciliation and agreed action while scrupulously avoiding the distinguishing tenets or nostrums of the established parliamentary parties. Blair, himself, claims to be inaugurating a popular politics 'reconciling themes which in the past have been wrongly regarded as antagonistic'. He prises politicians out of their old convictions to discover their unsuspected affinities. For the future lies in the cooperative exploitation of the 'knowledge economy', the joint fostering of British human resources and creativity. The plane is utopian; the end, in all possibility, 'a ballet dance of bloodless categories'.

The Third Way may seem a medley of incompatibilities or antinomies but it is surely designed variously to augment and strengthen the multilateral motivation and general support mobilized behind New Labour's central enterprise: the wilful recasting and re-branding of the old country'. Like Peter Wentworth, the Elizabethan tribune and archetypal liberal, Blair asserts: 'Behold I am as the new wine which hath no vent and bursteth the old vessels in sunder'.

XX

In yet another respect is Blair's way a liberal engagement: it seeks expansion not by conflict with but by rapprochement with rival forces. A central aim of New Labour is to subsume or 'swallow' other parties, individuals, or factions with kindred policies, outlooks or sympathies. Progressive, enlightened, encompassing, it hopes to dispense with the 'most certain enmities' of politics. As an irresistible persuasion and puissance it seeks to absorb footloose Social Democrats of the old Alliance or aberrant pro-European Tories — both detachable elements from larger formations — into a new broadbottom, even 'tesselated', national government — a process of gathering into 'the Big Tent' termed 'hoovering' by Peter Mandelson. The task of *this*, possibly the *last*, party, is to create a 'new country'. Only the Conservatives, quite unable to accept such a domination, such 'terminal inclusion', will remain outside, either in mute non-resistant Anglican subordination or as a residual English nationalist rump. The 'organic fissure' in the British party system which divides Labour from Liberal and gives the Conservative party ascendancy for a century will come to an end.

New Labour's landslide victory of 1997 was too decisive to make a realignment of parties possible or necessary. New Labour needed no help from the Liberal Democrats to sustain themselves in power. A coalition with Ashdown, the Liberal Democratic leader, proved unnecessary. For New Labour the prospect of a Lib-Lab, Centre-Left fusion remains only as an adumbration in their Project for the time to come. Yet there are those who consider that there is still an urgent need to leaven or animate the over-earnest, encumbered, indeed ponderous and unsuccessful party of Old Labour simply because without aeration, without spirit, it is unlikely to win governing majority again. To equip itself for victory as New Labour it needs what only liberalism can give it: a sense of moral energy and moral superiority, together with a mission to replace 'most certain enmities' with good feelings towards all. For is not liberalism, in the words of Ortega y Gasset, 'the supreme form of generosity', announcing, 'its determination to share existence with the enemy,' offering 'a method, a capacity to reconstruct within oneself the spiritual processes of others'? Liberalism claims to elevate everything that it touches and continues to monopolize the pulpits, ecclesiastical and secular. Indeed, is not its message recognizable as a kind of high-faluting Third Way?

Blair concedes that the beliefs of Liberalism have much in common with those of New Labour. At the heart of both is the rational, adapting individual accepting and absorbing the modern, the enlightened values and disparaging or dismissing the backward, the outdated, the residual. Both are given to rationalism in politics, believe, with Tom Paine, that 'man is man's enemy through a false system of government', actively seek to free mankind from the trammels of tradition. Each tends to idealism and harbours utopian tendencies. Each, from time to time, looks like the proverbial woodcock running about with the shell still on its head. Wherever his own essentially romantic, monocratic ventures in domestic or world politics may take him, Blair starts from liberal values. Coalition between a national party and a minor party with nothing much to offer but spirit, high-mindedness and anti-Tory animus remains projected as long as Blair aspires to comprehensive 'Gladstonian' leadership of a dominant Lib-Lab fusion, seeking, as 'the political wing of the British people', to establish not an alternative government but one 'that governs for a generation and changes Britain for good'.

There will be pickings for the Liberal Democrats in any political realignment, fulfilment and *réclame* for them in any new ascendancy clearly reflecting or endorsing a liberal social and political order through grand concordat. Liberals will prefer to see the grand incumbent, the prime mover, installed as a Jenkinsite First Pivot rather than as a Single Person Elective Dictator. As a party they are notably opportunistic, excessively enlightened about frontiers in One World, somewhat uninstructed in national self-understanding and not at all robust about the *patria*. They do not fuss about 'station and duties'; within the island, they are loth to respect 'any objective order antecedent to and superior to themselves'; they are, of course, much given to self-direction and individual choice and are very much at home in the swirl of modernity, change and fashion. They release more energy than they accumulate. In all these respects they do not differ very much from New Labour. Blair's liberal affinities are therefore quite appropriate.

Yet within Blair's 'matrix of possibilities' as a political leader, the role of archetypal liberal hero does not surely rank very high. Quite different modes of monocratic political being are more easily conjured up from or vested in aspects of his virtuosity: the Romantic in search of his 'occasion'; the Covenanted in search of his People; the Enlightened Despot seeking National Efficiency; the Elective Dictator mobilizing his Mountain; the President seeking his Presidency; the World-Besotted Statesman seeking celebrity; just possibly, a Legislator of the *nomos* of the earth; the Warlord of the Just War. But it is as none of these but as a liberal that the ground rises under his feet when he seeks to break the mould of British politics.

XXI

It is under the tutelage of Peter Mandelson, Roy Jenkins and others that he becomes the centre of the Project to transform the long-excluded Liberal-Left of British politics into a dominating, extruding Centre Coalition through which Liberal lineaments are clearly visible: serious consideration of Proportional Representation; abolition or re-modelling of the House of Lords; a favourable attitude towards 'Celtic' devolution; further absorption of a social democratic state into the European Union and so forth; above all, the installation of a leadership and party of Gladstonian scope and authority as a mainspring of progressive policies. It is the kind of party which might have been formed under the stimulus of Edwardian New Liberalism centring on a call for National Efficiency and jettisoning sectarianism, old loyalties and catch words in pursuit of that modernization which will secure a mastery of powers in a competitive world.

For Blair the liberal society from which he emerges remains formative and personally congenial. Self-disclosure, self-enactment, political performance all come naturally to him. He is in the van of things, dismissive of tradition and always seems ready to embrace the new. At home and abroad he is promiscuously open to innovation, rearrangement and reorientation. New Labour and Liberal Democrats are existentially un-Conservative. Blair shares the liberal desire to break out of the given social reality, the world as it has come to be. Both are potentially destructive of existing authorities and institutions. Both convert universal values into political ideals to which the given order is coldly and obtusely obstructive. Both believe in deep change not by political upheaval but by the application of passion-inspired or desire—stimulated reason to what perversely and irrationally prevails. Both Labour and Liberal are prone to what Santayana calls the 'illusion of the directive imagination', the belief that the world takes shape in response to human ideas and designs. In politics the daydream becomes reality; the spiritual value becomes the practical imperative and programme. 'The new minister is again a child ... He dreams of speeches applauded, measures passed, elections won ... and statues of oneself in public squares'. *Fortuna* smiles on prowess and the 'hand of history' lies on the politician's shoulder.

At the highest level liberalism develops a critique not only of the state but of politics itself. It tends to prefer a neutral state to a strong state and, according to Carl Schmitt, is reluctant to sacrifice life for it. It employs what Koselleck calls its own 'moral inner space', sitting in judgment upon the diurnal conduct of government. Initially its attack is too shallow to affect the struggle for power within the state or change the bases of the existing political culture. So in time it ceases to content itself with urging the moral against the political — there is a sense in which there is always a vein in liberal thought which negates the political — and develops its own high-minded and rational critiques of what is. It prides itself and contents itself with its own lofty self-consciousness, its elevated ethical superiorities and seeks to transform history into autonomous 'forensic process'. Moreover, liberalism emerges from this long dialogue not in pursuit so much of the democratic concept of a polity of rulers and ruled in unity as of a community of persons possessed of abstract rights.

Liberalism is not over-concerned with either the immanent or the concrete and tends to seek the resolution of the undetermined or the inexplicit, to forage in the forever extending field of possibilities. As a society it provides opportunities and occasions for self-directing, self-fulfilling individuals seeking creativity, vocation, powers or wealth. Emerging from their matrices in all their variety they are preoccupied with ideas or ideals and with the political rationalism which is necessary for the construction of their alternatives to extant reality. Theirs may not be benign activities, involving as they do the destruction of existing traditions, moralities and orders of conveniences. Rarely, it calls into being — and action — the heroic energy of an archetypal figure, like Blair, elevated, passionate, possibly charismatic, who seizes the opportunity or the 'occasion' to impose his imperatives on his milieu or setting and achieve his goals or dreams. Even, however, if the liberal is engaged like Prometheus in stealing fire, his mode soon ceases to be 'millenarian'. Far from being chained to a rock, as 'celebrity', he has little difficulty in insinuating himself into both civil society and the political order. Diluting enmity and deploring inveteracy, face, presence and persona are assimilated to the 'animated moderation' of modern liberalism.

Blair's is a utopian *patria* of liberal provenance, a rational reconstruction to replace what has obstructively come to be, to provide a political model for a time to come. Against 'the forces of conservatism', a sustained turn of the imagination conjures up from universalized aspiration and dream, a guide rather than a model for the future. For perfectibility is ultimate not proximate. Felicity is attained by liberals in the progression, in the travelling not the arriving, in the suffusing elevation of spirit derived from the pursuit of the elusive, barely defined transforming idea created by the professed 'political arm of the British people as a whole'.

The agency, the party of New Labour, looks not to institutional inheritance, to character, destiny or fate or to historical forces but to renovation of spirit, remobilization of energies from which will emerge a 'new patriotism' focussed on 'the potential we can fulfil in the future'. The *patria* is not only something to be projected, made and, above all, to be presented and defined in terms of imagination and rationalism; it is also an enterprise to be managed. A modern agency or instrumentality without discursive historical roots or myth, it is the product of will and dominance within a particular party ascendancy. The aim is a conventional one: the survival of Britain not as a power among powers in the world but as an important constituent of a highly active liberal international community. To that end it claims to be a moral entity independent of all traditions. At present it seems to operate in no other dialectic than what may be teased out of the Third Way. The party's watchwords constantly heap Pelion on Ossa: renewal is constantly urged upon what is already evoked as 'a young and vibrant country'.

Without the presumption of the oscillation of two 'great parties' alternating forever and a day in the light or darkness of office, futurity promises an uninterrupted progressive movement to what looks like an insular liberal utopia. The infusion of liberal spirit, idealistic, imaginative and possibly romantic, into a dominant Lib-Lab fusion as projected or realized must strengthen the ethical framework for an active, perhaps venturesome conscience in search of oppressions and iniquities outside the moralizing island much taken up with what Francis Hirst calls 'the higher considerations' in a wider world. According to Blair, celebrating Kosovo, 'the age of the truly liberal and humanitarian war has already dawned'. Virtue is already running amuk through the veins of the 'coalitions of the willing' mustered from such active, ethical *patriae* as may be available in the 'international community'. Thus the Labour party, at times, as the unpatriotic party disprized, becomes under a new persona the proponent of an 'enlightened patriotism' and duly appoints what Britain has never known, a Minister of Patriotism. The impalpable *patria* may occupy a variety of locations. In placing his projected reorientation in a utopia — no place — in the future, abandoning existent reality and transcending all ideology, indeed confining himself to a glossary, Blair converts his renovating *pars pro toto* into re-enactment of dream or wish-picture. Everything, however, is to be conducted perfectly reasonably. Upheaval is forsworn. Electoral victories will, it is hoped, transform the British Constitution into an effective executive of a utopian *sub-patria*.

XXII

It is a *leitmotiv* of this essay that Tony Blair, New Labour, twice the overwhelming choice of Labour is no more of that 'great movement' than, as is sometimes alleged, he is a crypto-Conservative Prime Minister; that as an emergent leading politician he evinces attitudes, beliefs, policies and conduct indicating that essentially his politics are liberal. According to the fourth and fifth meanings given in the Shorter OED the political 'liberal' is one who is 'free from narrow prejudice ... open to the reception of new ideas and proposals of reform ... opposite to Conservative'. These meanings convey no 'public doctrine'; they do presumably subsume 'liberal values'. Moreover, while Blair may bear many of the marks of a liberal protagonist in politics they are neither deep nor indelible simply because liberalism is characteristically tenuous and indeterminate and as a universal external critique of a given order, necessarily singular, particularized, and obtusely resistant, makes only a shallow impression. Nevertheless, the society from which Blair springs may well be designated as 'liberal'.

So too may his values and imperatives — which he seeks to promote either in domestic politics through his Third Way or, in international politics, through his 'Doctrine of the International

Community', post-Kosovo. His systematic recourse to political rationalism to remake historical or political reality is a liberal process long before it is socialist. It is this activity which ensures that much of the world is not merely transmitted to us from the past but is created anew. Thus Blair characteristically operates under that 'illusion of the directive imagination' to which Santayana maintains liberals are particularly prone to rely in order to set in motion rational plans to amend, transform, undermine or destroy the repugnant reality around them. The romanticism which sparks on occasions Blair's 'eye-catching' initiatives has its seed-bed in the indeterminacy, the world of open possibilities, nourished by liberalism. It stimulates and facilitates subjective wilful and wishful escapes from vaporous inertia and indecision towards the creation of new realities, points of departure, new milieus or fields of activity for the egotistic, liberal free will. In moral or aesthetic elevation these ventures are startlingly liberal. In the words of Mannheim, they spark off 'rational conceptions to be set against evil realities'. They may be *en route* to some utopian way-station in liberal unilinear history. This is history that Blair can accept.

Blair's wars are, as we have seen, 'just', liberal wars. His attempts to assist American Neo-Conservatives at 'nation-building' in Afghanistan and Iraq have been labelled 'liberal imperialist'. His alternatives to the given British *patria* are rational and remote: on the one hand, he reverts to the progressive eighteenth-century concept of 'the citizen of the world'; on the other, to a loyalty to some Continental fatherland. These are still figments of the liberal imagination. As is his utopian British sub-*patria*, furnished with a Minister of Patriotism. There is no *demos* behind any of them. The only *demos* behind Blair is British but that serves to empower him at the polls rather than patriotise him.

Above all, Blair's political persona is liberal, 'open' and receptive. Indeed, he personifies the idea of 'good will turned doctrinaire': successfully he contrives unofficiously, if not unstrenuously, to present a sustained front of cordiality, amiability and the sense of 'well-met'. Like Browning's 'Last Duchess' he likes whatever he looks on and his looks go everywhere. Like Clinton, Blair rises politically by a capacity to display liberality; studied charm; systematic recourse to porcupine, instant rebuttal in diurnal politics; ruthlessness; a certain lack of cultural discrimination and of political rigour and consistency; above all, to popularity. 'Popularity', meaning 'the fact or condition of being admired, approved or beloved by the people' entered the English language in the mid-seventeenth century. Then it meant a reputation for 'patriotism' and a power through it to influence people. Since then 'popularity' has become dissociated from the patriot and is more commonly applied to 'the celebrity'.

But whether attributed to Blair as 'patriot' or 'celebrity' it is popularity that enables him politically to commune so effectively with others so that he considers that he is in a position to lay down a new sediment of common opinion upon which an alternative national consensus may be constructed to replace the old coherences of traditional Britain now overdue for re-branding. This, it is said, he seeks to establish not by ideology, not by radical action — though this is to be 'the century of radicalism' — but through personal example, by preaching, teaching, social controls — all by charisma interpenetrated — possibly, by micro-management of the focus groups or re-charging the educational curriculum, thus stimulating innovatory popular thought, beliefs and such conjectural narrative of past and future as may continue to sustain this providential regime and its renovating consensus. This is the liberal Blair doing what he enjoys doing: addressing not Parliament but the public.

The question which arises is how the benign, indeterminate Blair, coming to office with eirenic, utopian leanings, subjectively develops seemingly 'without uncertainties, mysteries, doubts' not only such monocratic and decisive tendencies but also looses with almost Palmerstonian *esprit* such a string of imperative policies, innovatory or renovatory — together with the *personae* to go with them — at home and abroad. The liberal who deprecates the politics of power shows that he can thrive on them, make a virtue of them and display a fecundity of initiatives which have their impulsions not within the fertile liberal pluralisms within the Cabinet, party or Parliament but within an unrevealed Caesarist command structure sustained by largely incognisant and innominate, loosely structured posse or *comitatus* of advisers, intelligencers, prompters and minders. The exponent of inclusive politics who dissolves hostility in irresistible affability, reduces serried political convictions to idle dreams and speculations, continues indefatigably to expand 'the tendency to agree' but himself develops a determining passion for the politics of ultimate moral ends. Moreover, going well beyond the purviews of liberalism, he identifies *the foe*, the absolute enemy and reveals a destructive dynamism in a personal pursuit of terrestrial virtues.

So the rational pursuit of liberal ends leads to the installation of a personal political dominance. What emerges is not the co-operation of the persuaded but the autonomy of an egotistic will occasionally illumined by a romanticism which cannot but define political activity in terms of the mobile self forever seeking not liberal incrementalism or heuristic prudence but the rapid realisation of the universalized moral values, displacement of old orders, institutions and practices, movement on to higher planes — primarily through sustained criticism of what is. Singular political drive forces its way through liberal indeterminacy openly to embrace adversarial politics, not so much against liberalism which remains within Blair's matrix of possibilities, but against its existential enemies, 'the forces of conservatism', notably English Toryism. The conscience of the prime mover, previously influenced by other intimations of 'the right thing to do', assumes a preferred position. Romanticism may still embellish the political actor but it is as decisionist that he dominates. The popular, the consensual, the righteous and the rational, cohere to sustain the single legitimacy of the monocratic Outsider.

What this signifies is that the political, for the time being, triumphs over the liberal. As leader of a mainstream party intent on rapidly becoming 'the political wing of the British people', Blair cares less and less for liberal institutions critical of and perhaps inimical to the power of the state. For Blair, conceiving of himself as the Legislator as well as the Executive, Parliament with its checks and balances must often seem an impediment. It would seem that he needs it less for assisting will-formation than for acclamation and endorsement; that debates, far from eliciting *veritas*, produce congeries of opinion which inhibit or impair what unity may be achieved between ruler and ruled. Clearly, Blair prefers Parliament to be a place where decisions have already been taken. Little wonder that under his regime the House of Commons is said by the Father of the House to have 'atrophied' and the Lords, consigned — despite recalcitrance — to a kind of constitutional limbo. The Cabinet no longer acts as a plural executive and party is subordinated to a Caesarean persona and his cronies.

As Weber requires, Blair is trained for leadership in a liberal democratic Parliamentary arena. And it is liberalism which provides the rules for his struggle for power as well as extramurally endowing him with values. But it is double-barrelled *demos* that gives him the near-absolute authority in Parliament and enables him to depart from liberalism awhile and embrace adversary politics controlled and conducted by a single pair of hands. For he finds that it is not liberal discussion that will realize 'what Tony wants' but existentialist decision within his own personal public doctrines solidifying memorably into viable prejudice. As the People's Arm, the erstwhile 'congenital liberal' enters fully into political conflict, identifies his mortal enemies and brings into being, as fate or fortune demands, new ruling *personae*, new monocracies from his matrix of possibilities. Outside the real, outside the *ipso facto*, he continues as a romantic, to make up his own reality as he goes along.

What we see in Blair is not the dissolution of a political faith. He is conditioned by liberal milieus but no faith binds or looses him. He acknowledges no established public doctrine. Identifiable party Liberals, as such, characteristically opportunist rejoicing in by-elections, concentrating upon the miscellaneous and the multilateral, seeking momentarily to draw in the uninitiated, the unpolitical, the alienated and the alien, seem intent on forming or raising a mêlée rather than anything Blair is likely to recognize as a 'community'. Blair observes liberal values, liberal ethics. He shares the liberal predisposition to agree with others. Like all liberals he is much engaged on critiques of what has come to be. He is happy that liberals supply him with the rules of the political game as long as *demos* provides him with the *ultima ratio*, the unanswerable argument. But liberalism does not furnish him with a political faith.

Blair then is no lapsed liberal — there is no public doctrine to abandon. Nor is he what Michael Oakeshott might have called a liberal *manqué*, a failed liberal. Rather he finds that liberalism itself is becoming inappropriate to his changing political role. As decisionist innovator and exponent of the liberal 'just war' he finds that liberalism cannot cope with real politics. What Blair seeks to resolve as virtuous warlord or decisionist statesman cannot always be conclusively settled by 'a tendency to agree', constructive engagement, 'communicative rationality', disciplined universal pragmatism. 'Ideal speech situations' are few. For, as Weber maintains, there is no overarching system of higher values through which lower sublunary values and imperatives may assuredly be brought into harmony. When Blair ends the discourse, asserts monocratic authority as decisionist prime mover, cuts his way through the confabulations of politics to recognize what he considers to be the *ipso facto*, there is no transfiguration. All he does is to assume another 'nature' from his *matrix of possibilities*. As a discursive romantic he is accustomed to moving from one state of mind to another expressing and presenting them as the occasion demands. To none of them is the protean Blair committed. They all have their particular uses within a dominance.

SOCIETAS

essays in political and cultural criticism

Contemporary public debate has been impoverished by two competing trends. On the one hand the increasing commercialization of the media has meant that in-depth commentary has given way to the ten-second soundbite. On the other hand the explosion of scholarly knowledge has led to intense specialization, so that academic discourse has ceased to be comprehensible. As a result writing on politics and culture is either superficial or baffling.

This was not always so — especially for politics. The high point of the English political pamphlet was the seventeenth century, when a number of small printer-publishers responded to the political ferment of the age with an outpouring of widely-accessible pamphlets and tracts. Indeed Imprint Academic publishes facsimile C17th. reprints under the banner 'The Rota'.

In recent years the tradition of the political pamphlet has declined—with most publishers rejecting anything under 100,000 words. The result is that many a good idea ends up drowning in a sea of verbosity. However the digital press makes it possible to re-create a more exciting age of publishing. *Societas* authors are all experts in their own field, but the essays are for a general audience. Each book can be read in an evening. The books are available retail at the price of £8.95/$17.90 each, or on bi-monthly subscription for only £5/$10. Details: **www.imprint.co.uk/societas**

IMPRINT ACADEMIC, PO Box 200, Exeter, EX5 5YX, UK
Tel: (0)1392 841600   Fax: (0)1392 841478   sandra@imprint.co.uk